A HIKER'S COMPANION

12,000 Miles of Trail-Tested Wisdom

A HIKER'S COMPANION

12,000 Miles of Trail-Tested Wisdom

*Cindy Ross &
Todd Gladfelter*

The Mountaineers/Seattle

For all our hiking companions.
Thanks for the memories.

Published by The Mountaineers
1011 SW Klickitat Way, Seattle, Washington 98134

Published simultaneously in Canada by Douglas & McIntyre, Ltd., 1615 Venables Street, Vancouver, B.C. V5L 2H1

Published simultaneously in Great Britain by Cordee, 3a DeMontfort Street, Leicester, England, LE1 7HD

Manufactured in the United States of America

Edited by Kris Fulsaas
Drawings by Cindy Ross
Cover design by Watson Graphics
Book design and typography by Hargrave Design
Cover photo by Dan Peha; inset by the authors

The following trademarks appear in this book: NutraSweet, M&Ms, BakePacker, Band-Aids, Svea.

Library of Congress Cataloging-in-Publication Data
Ross, Cindy.
        The hiker's companion: 12,000 miles of trail-tested wisdom/ by Cindy Ross and Todd Gladfelter.
        p. cm.
        Includes index.
        ISBN 0-89886-353-8
        1. Hiking.   2. Backpacking.   I. Gladfelter, Todd.   II. Title.
GV199.4.R67   1993
796.5'1–dc20   92-46568
                                                            CIP

Acknowledgments

Our log house has an open design; because of this, you can hear everything anywhere you go. It's not designed for privacy, nor for writing books. When Todd cared for our children while I worked on this book, I had to resort to wearing the tight ear protectors that he uses with his chainsaw because I heard too much giggling, storybook reading, Raffi, and rattles. It was too painful; I couldn't stand to miss the fun that was going on. I had to get out of the house.

We were fortunate to find two babysitters who deeply loved our children. When Susie Braun came to watch our kids, I retired to our log sauna to write, and sat on a folding chair right smack in the doorway because in the rest of the building it was too dark to see. I put my pen down only when Bryce cried too hard and too long for a mother to bear. When Amy Heintzelman babysat, I dropped the children off at her house and drove a quarter mile down the dirt road to the state game lands parking lot. There, I spread my various papers out on the seat, dashboard, and floor. What an office! Thank you, girls, for caring and for helping.

Then I discovered late in the game that I needed to put this manuscript on a computer disk. I did not own, nor know how to operate, a computer. I am no perfect secretary, as I type with only a few fingers, and I haven't memorized the keyboard, so I must watch the keys to type after I read a phrase. My friend, Andrianne, was generous enough to allow me to use her computer—which she herself did not know how to operate—for the task. We were often on the phone bugging my friend Marilyn Faughner about how to get something back that I thought I had erased. To help the process along, she unselfishly helped transcribe my typed pages onto her computer at work to insure that I met deadlines. She went in to work early, stayed late, and typed during lunch and on some Saturdays. Girls, there's no way this book could have been made without you. Thank you.

Contents

Part I:
BEFORE YOU GO

Part II:
OUT THERE

Part III:
PLAYING IT SAFE

Part IV:
EXTRAS

Preface

*W*ithin *The Hiker's Companion* you will find hard-earned knowledge, hints and tips, and a lot of good stories. Stories of how we learned to be backpackers. *The Hiker's Companion* does not profess to be the bible of hiking. No profound truths or indisputable facts are found here. It is just the humble opinion of two seasoned hikers.

We have taught a hiking/backpacking class at a nearby college for nearly a decade. As we teach, we frequently pause to tell a good story. We feel there's nothing like a real-life example to bring home and illustrate a point. We believe learning should be fun and painless, if possible. We strive to get our information across in such a way that the information is absorbed without the student even realizing it. We always say that our students learn from all of our past 12,000 miles of mistakes and experience—that they are much farther down the road because we have shared what we learned.

Because most of you can't take our course, hear our stories, and learn from us one-on-one, we have written this book. We have a lot to share from all those miles. We think it will help many of you to learn to love hiking deeply and learn the sport with greater ease because of it. Think of this book not as a hiking bible but as a companion—two friendly companions, Todd and me—sharing our hiking lives and all that we know with you.

Introduction

The Philosophy of Hiking

*W*hat makes a good hiker? The best hikers, and the ones who love the sport the most, have learned to feel very comfortable on the trail with themselvesand with the natural environment. This can only happen after you spend a lot of time out there, once the outdoors begins to feel like home. And it doesn't stem from having the right gear, necessarily. It's having the right head—a good attitude, and a positive frame of mind.

Much of the following wisdom comes from the mind of our good friend, Warren Doyle, who completed the entire Appalachian Trail (AT) seven times, and created the Appalachian Trail Institute, a program designed to give prospective hikers an honest, realistic idea of what's involved with hiking from Georgia to Maine. We share the same beliefs.

Don't fight the trail. You have to flow with it. You can't make a mountain any less steep or an afternoon any cooler or the day any longer, so don't waste your energy complaining. Time and distance and terrain and the trail itself cannot be changed. You have to change yourself. You have to adapt your mind, heart, and soul to the trail. For every five days on the trail, you can expect one day to be uncomfortably wet, one day to be uncomfortably dry, one day to be uncomfortably hot, one day to be uncomfortably cold, and one day to be comfortable.

Don't expect nature to respect your manmade comfort level and your desire to control your environment. In our desire to avoid discomfort we may become more uncomfortable. Leave your cultural level of comfort at home. Forget about your material wants. Just concentrate on your physical and spiritual needs. Yes, you can wear one T-shirt the entire journey; you don't have to take showers; you can survive on one hot meal a day; you don't need a roof and walls around you at night.

Leave your emotional fat at home as well. Feel free to laugh and to cry, to feel lonely and to feel afraid, to feel socially irresponsible and to feel foolish, and to feel free. Rediscover your childhood. Play the game of the trail. Roll with the punches and learn to laugh in the face of adversity.

Be optimistic. Things could always be worse. Don't become mired in the swamp of sorrow. Some thoughts to have in your head: Upon reaching the top of the mountain—"Gee, I'm here already." Upon reaching your campsite—"Golly, that day went fast." Upon starting your hike—"It's going to hurt and be hard, but I'm still going to enjoy it." After your first week on the trail—"Gosh, this isn't as hard as I thought it would be." During your sixth straight day of rain—"At least the springs aren't dry." During your third week of drought—"At least I don't have to put on wet socks in the morning." During the second straight week of mosquitos/black flies—"At least they're not wasps."

This all sounds like good advice for our daily lives, doesn't it? That's one of the reasons hiking means so much to us. Trail life teaches us how to live all the other parts of our lives, too. The most important lessons we have learned in life the trail has taught us.

PART

BEFORE YOU GO

▲ ▲ ▲ ▲ ▲ ▲ ▲ ▲ ▲

CHAPTER 1

Gear

▲ ▲ ▲ ▲ ▲ ▲ ▲ ▲ ▲

*A*lthough we are starting with gear, we do not feel it is the most important aspect of the sport. Quite the contrary! Grandma Gatewood, at the age of sixty-five, hiked the entire Appalachian Trail with a shower curtain for a ground cloth (no sleeping pad!) and sneakers for footgear. One hiker on the AT was lugging a golf bag instead of a fancy internal frame pack. Your gear is partially responsible for getting you down the trail and keeping you on it (and out of the repair shop), so good-quality gear is usually worth the money you must pay for it. It can last a lifetime or close to it. Once you find a backpack that fits you well, and goes on all sorts of adventures with you, it can become your dear friend and be very difficult to replace with a more modern and advanced piece.

That's what happened to Todd, being the tenacious German that he is. His vintage framepack served him faithfully for 5,000 miles. Years ago it was considered *the* pack to own. When he learned he would field-test a new pack for *Backpacker* magazine on our 750-mile traverse of the Sierra Nevada, he was not only nervous, he was heartsick. In time, he came to love his new pack and stored his old one away for the kids. (Right! To them his old framepack will seem as dated as the old beltless, cotton duck rucksacks from the Fifties are to us.)

We are not "gear heads," personally. We don't buy every new item that technology puts on the market. Our personal values are more simplistic in nature. Any new gear we have, we usually acquired from lengthy field tests—making the gear so ingrained with our sweat that the manufacturers didn't want it back.

Bear in mind that if you are into acquiring equipment it will not make you a better hiker or backpacker. And it is not necessary in order to have a good time. Poor gear, on the other hand, does have a way of testing your good humor.

Warren Doyle advises his students to go out and buy the cheapest pair of boots a discount store has to offer. The number of replacement pairs you must buy still won't add up to the cost of better-quality expensive boots, he says. But vinyl boots almost crippled Bill Irwin, who, with his seeing-eye dog, Orient, became the first blind person to hike the entire length of the AT. His feet ached so badly and were blistered to the point where he had to get off the trail for days to heal and look for new "good" boots.

We've taken our 4-H group of twelve-year-old boys out and they sloshed around in rain gear made of garbage bags with holes cut out for their heads and arms and they couldn't have been happier. Those same kids toted backpacks that were really pieces of luggage their parents selected for them (despite our instructions as leaders) so that they could be used for something "useful" later on. And the thick, heavy cotton-flannel sleeping bags with the hunters-and-pointer-dogs patterns rolled up in unruly bundles and tied on haphazardly with binder's twine and hitting the kids' legs as they walked never once interfered with their near-constant chatter and jokes.

As we said in the Introduction, much of your success in this sport is derived from your mindset. As adults, however, many of us are no longer equipped with the ability to ignore such discomforts brought on by poor gear. For us, it is more necessary now to begin with all those bases covered.

Purchase quality equipment from a reputable supplier. The comfort level is far superior to inexpensive, poorly made items found in discount stores. Find an outfitter and patronize it. Nothing can compare to personally trying on a piece of equipment and having it adjusted to your individual body frame. Hopefully, your salesperson will know a lot about the particular kind of gear he or she sells and will know how to insure a good fit. Sometimes you wonder, however, if he or she sold cars or encyclopedias door-to-door before landing this job. Do not rely on such salespeople. Educate yourself on how your boots should fit or how a loaded pack should feel. Salespeople will sometimes try to sell you what is selling, what is popular. Try to determine beforehand what your personal needs are and what you plan on doing with the gear so that you don't purchase more or less than you need. For example, if you know you love to hike in all seasons, snowy winters included, and can only afford to purchase one pair of boots, a lightweight, fabric-type boot would *not* be your best choice, but perhaps a medium-weight, leather boot would. No salesperson can tell you what your needs are. Do your homework before you go to buy.

I was in a sporting goods store once and overheard a salesman trying to talk a girl into buying some high-topped leather hunting boots because, he said, along with their height, the Gore-Tex waterproof liner would keep her feet dry. When he went behind the curtain to get another size, I whispered, "No boot will stay waterproof for long. Leather needs to breathe, to begin with. And Gore-Tex ceases to perform when it gets dirty. Can you think of many places that get dirtier when you hike than your feet?"

Another thing that's nice about purchasing good-quality gear is that the manufacturer almost always has a lifetime warranty attached. There's been many a long-distance hiker who has frantically called his or her pack or boot manufacturer from the trail with a horror story of failed equipment and has had it replaced in short order, no matter how many miles were on the equipment.

There is more than one good reason to take care of your gear. First, it's expensive to replace. A piece of good equipment could last your lifetime if you don't abuse it and wear it out prematurely. It could make your trip more comfortable. Anyone who's spent the night in a leaky tent knows the importance of a good seam-seal job. And if something should break, it's not likely that you'll have a spare along. But most importantly, under adverse conditions your gear could save your life. Besides your wits, it's all you have with which to survive when you're in the bush.

When you go into a store that sells gear, take your business elsewhere if the salespeople do not want to take the time to fit the pack to your body, or allow you to crawl inside a sleeping bag, or light a stove, or set up a tent to actually see the interior. Hiking and backpacking gear is not cheap. You should be fully aware of what you are buying. Maybe laying in that tent will make you realize that a two-person tent is definitely too small for you to want to spend any amount of time in it with anyone, no matter how light it is. Or maybe that winter sleeping bag is cut so narrowly, to make up for its weight, that it does not allow you to bend your knee inside and, hence, not allow you to sleep the way you enjoy. How else would you discover this if you couldn't get inside of it?

Backpacks

Let's start with the equipment you absolutely must have before you can venture out. There are basically two kinds of overnight backpacks used on the trail. An external frame pack is designed to carry heavy loads over long distances. They are especially good on fairly open trails where not a lot of bushwhacking needs to be done. They are very comfortable in warm weather because the rigid frame keeps the pack away from your back, enabling your perspiration to evaporate.

Internal frame packs are less rigid than externals and ride very close to your body, offering a lot of stability and balance. They are best suited for sports like cross-country skiing and rock climbing. Their body-hugging, slim profile make them perform very well in tight places and heavy brush. They are very hot in warm weather, however.

Today's move is toward internal frame packs. They are the hottest sellers. Consumers are asking for them and salespeople are pushing them. We personally swear by externals.

Remember one thing: you *must* put that pack on your back in the store—have it *totally* adjusted to your individual body frame and fully loaded before making your decision. Most packs today come with a myriad of different adjustments, making you wish the pack came with its own representative to help you figure it out. But taking the time to fit it properly makes all the difference in the world.

I've worn packs that were simply not sized for my frame. Many of today's packs claim to accommodate a wide range of body torso lengths, often 5 feet 5 inches to 6 feet and over. Since I am 5 feet 6 inches tall—at the low end of the scale—I often cannot get them sized down low enough to fit me comfortably under a load.

Your pack's weight must be distributed in the right proportion (most of it on your hips). Your shoulder straps should go from your shoulder into your pack at the right angle. If a pack fits well, a

lot of weight in it will not cause it to make you feel uncomfortable, at least not while walking around the store.

After the half dozen different adjustments are made to fit the pack to you, have the salesperson load it up to about fifty pounds. You can tell a lot about a pack when it is under weight. Nearly any pack feels fine if it's light, even one that does not fit you at all. Put a lot of weight in it, however, and it can turn your trip into hell.

Place a sleeping bag from the store on the bottom, then boots and climbing ropes or the like to get your weight high. Now how does it feel? You say you never plan on carrying a pack that heavy? It's hard to say what trails you will be led down someday. Todd's pack weighed ninety pounds on an overnighter once because he was carrying diapers, a few gallons of water (we were in the desert), and gear for three (I had the baby).

We've had seventy pounds for a winter overnighter carrying homemade glass-bottled beer, a whole chicken, and firewood. Also, all you have to do is go for an extended trip of five to seven days, or hike in a dry stretch with no water for a day or two, and your pack can easily hit fifty pounds.

For the same reason, look for a backpack that has a slightly larger capacity than what you may expect to need. It is much easier to carry less in a bigger pack than to cram more into a too-small pack. We personally like the feature of a lot of outside pockets as opposed to the one large sack of some internals with virtually no external pockets.

Find your hip bones. Your waist belt should sit right above and on them. Bend over, hunch your pack up, and cinch your waist belt tight. Then, when you stand upright and the weight settles down, your belt will not slide lower than it should.

Most of your pack's weight should be on your hips. I had a friend who hiked 400 miles on the Appalachian Trail without *any* weight on his hips. When I saw his belt loosely sliding around his torso, I was shocked. I quickly showed him a better way. It revolutionized backpacking for him. He foolishly thought his belt was merely for keeping his pack from swaying around. Never once had he complained about his load, or I could have helped him sooner!

Many greenhorns tighten their shoulder straps way too tight. Only tighten them enough to keep your pack close and stable. You can play with the adjustments while you hike, but keep these basic principles in mind.

Packing Your Pack

When you pack your backpack, aim to keep your heaviest items as high as possible and as close to your back as possible. Sleeping bags usually go on the bottom, then your clothes, food, and the tent. If you have an internal frame pack, pad the rigid, angular objects, like your stove, so they don't poke you in the back. Your water bottles and gas bottles should be on the outside to minimize leakage. You can purchase chalk bags that climbers use to keep their hands dry and clip them onto your pack with a carabiner for carrying fuel or water bottles. The bottles fit snugly and won't sway when you walk.

My friend Nancy carried her fuel bottle inside her pack, as she had no external pockets. The rubber gasket became brittle and cracked one day, leaking gas onto our food—our only food left until our food pickup at the end of that long, hungry day. We had to eat the crackers and belched up disgusting gasoline breath all day long.

We like to put items in outside pockets that could be wet and, hence, wet our other gear that needs to be kept dry: items like the water bag, our rain gear, and the pack cover. We also like to keep them handy so they can be grabbed in a hurry.

The front pocket on some externals or the lid on some internals can serve as a "purse" to carry items like a hairbrush, toothpaste, a flashlight, toilet paper, hair twisties, tampons, bug repellent, and lip screen, perhaps all in their own ditty bag.

If space is really tight, there is a variety of gear that can be hung on the outside. Besides your fuel bottle, your shovel for digging latrine holes can go there, your cord, and your cup and spoon (with a hole drilled through the spoon handle). Shower hooks are good for this and alligator clips (also called "roach clips" by those who used to smoke marijuana in their juvenile days) are good for drying wet socks as you hike. The clips hold fabric in their jaws extremely tightly. They can be purchased at hardware stores. Todd also hooks some rubber bands and twisties onto a shower hook, and attaches a few spare clevis pins and a GI can opener as zipper pulls. The day will surely come when you will need this stuff but, in the meantime, you will at least look like a seasoned backpacker.

We like to carry a fanny pack and wear it in the front. In it I carry my camera and extra lens and film, a whistle, my map/guidebook in a zip-lock plastic bag, and a wallet or a zip-lock bag containing money and ID. If I ever leave my pack or become separated from it, I always have my most important possessions, things which will enable me to get help should my pack be stolen.

Pack Hints and Tips

Many hikers start off carrying much more weight than is comfortable and often more than their bodies can carry safely without harming them. A good rule of thumb when deciding on your load is to aim roughly for one-fifth to one-fourth of your body weight. You can increase this to as much as one-third as you grow stronger. All those extra items of convenience you think you're adding may mean inconvenience when the total weight is tallied.

Men who are tall and need a large pack but are on the thin side may have trouble with their hip belts fitting too loosely, especially if a hiker is on the trail for many months and begins to lose weight and body fat. A couple of small pieces of foam padding can be used

to take up the space. A rolled sweater can be used to make do on the trail also, although it is much more unruly.

To avoid losing a split ring, exchange the flimsy ones that come on your pack with tight, strong ones available at a hardware store.

Losing gear on the trail can be the cause of much inconvenience. A forgotten spoon or misplaced pocketknife can easily be lost and left among leaves. Every item in your pack has a specific and important purpose and doubles are not usually carried. One way of minimizing your chances is to leave the pocket zipper or flap open on your pack when removing items from it. That way, before shouldering your pack and leaving your lunch spot or campsite, you will notice if a particular pocket has been left open. If it is, something is missing from that pocket and you'll know to take a quick look around before leaving. It is much easier to take the time to do this than to backtrack many miles later in search of the missing item.

If it looks like rain when you're going to bed, bring in all the items that you may need for the early morning: maps and guidebook to examine the next day's route, rain gear, and, depending on conditions, breakfast. Always cover your pack before turning in for the night, even if the stars are out. The sky could easily cloud over and bring showers, and your sleep be disturbed to perform the task. It also protects the pack from dew and deters some animals from investigating its contents. It can at least act as an alarm if a critter is trying to enter.

If keeping your pack light is of importance to you, look at each piece of gear and see if you can find a lighter one to replace it with, or find a way to make that particular piece of gear lighter. It may seem extreme, but ounces add up to pounds. Some hikers trim the extra-wide borders on maps, cut the handle down on their toothbrush or drill holes in it, take off unused pockets, cuffs, and belt loops, and use plastic spoons and cups instead of metal.

Establish a routine for fitting your pack each time you put it on. Loosen the shoulder, load-lifter, and hip-stabilizer straps slightly. Bend your knees, swing the pack up onto your thigh, and slide under the shoulder straps in one quick motion. Lean forward and cinch the waistbelt. Stand up, settle the pack onto your hips, and pull the shoulder straps snug. Buckle the sternum strap, then tighten the load-lifters and hip-stabilizer straps to lessen the pack's tendency to sway or pull you backward. Ease a bit of slack into the shoulder straps so you can shrug your shoulders a little.

Your pack will have a longer life if you keep it cleaned and repaired. After a trip, unzip all packets and compartments and shake out any crumbs, dirt, sand, or trash. The interior can be sponged out with mild soap and warm water. The ultraviolet rays of direct sunlight can deteriorate synthetic fibers so avoid this if possible. Instead, dry it in an airy place.

Between trips, check for wear and tear, and replace worn clevis pins and split rings. If the nylon is fraying, melt the edges with a match or a lighter. Sew tears with a heavy-duty needle and upholstery thread. If stitching on the hipbelt or straps is loosening, sew it yourself or take it to a cobbler for repair. Packs should be stored in a cool and dry place to avoid mildew growth.

Sleeping Bags and Pads

Mummy sleeping bags are the warmest bags available because their design has the least amount of air space for your body to heat up. That's all we use now. As a kid, the big rectangular cotton bags were standard fare. I used to wonder why I was always so cold, especially my feet. There was so much more air space to heat up. And I more than likely had wet cotton socks on, too.

Mummy bags are also designed with hoods and drawstrings, which help to keep in your precious body heat, because 87 percent of your entire body's heat can be lost through your bare head. When it's very cold out, I pull my cords the tightest they will go until only a peephole remains to breathe through. My nose still gets so very cold that it keeps me awake. And even though they say not to put your nose or mouth inside because of all the moisture in your breath going into your bag, I cannot help it. It's either that, or I get no sleep.

Most mummy bags have a boxed foot section where the insulation is kept firmly in place, insuring that your feet are kept toasty warm. Most mummy bags are also constructed with a differential cut where the inner lining is smaller than the outer lining, so the insulation cannot be compressed from the inside.

Ounce for ounce, down is a better insulator but it compresses easily, making its insulation very low underneath your body. But down bags are easier to pack, stuffing down to an incredibly small size, and are extremely light. Much effort must be put into keeping a down bag dry since they take days to dry out on the trail.

When I was getting into backpacking in my mid- to late teens, my girlfriend and I came up with what we thought was a great idea for acquiring down. We were sewing a lot of our gear from kits. The contents contained plastic bags packed with down for stuffing jackets and sleeping bags. How could we get our own supply? There was a waterfowl area nearby where hunting was opened during a particular time of the year. Our plan was to make lots of loaves of zucchini and pumpkin bread and a big thermos of coffee. We'd put down the tailgate of my friend's pickup in the parking lot and while we chatted with the hunters over refreshments, we'd pluck their birds of the down! We also thought we'd begin to raise geese in our backyards for their down and sell it to the kit manufacturers. What an easy way to make a living. Why hadn't anyone thought of it? Neither plan materialized. As we grew more educated in the natural world, we learned that the geese would not have done well at all in the moderate, temperate climate of Pennsylvania. Geese need to live in the cold north to acquire sufficient down. For young greenhorns, though, these were pretty creative ideas!

These days we pretty much stick to synthetics for insulation. Synthetics are bulkier and harder to compress than down but they are easier to wash, faster to dry, much less expensive, and retain some of their warmth when wet. If you plan to backpack in a climate where there is much precipitation, it may be a better choice to pack a synthetic warm-when-wet bag.

A sleeping bag with a full-length two-way zipper is especially nice in warm weather when you could use the extra ventilation control down at your feet. Some nights are merely too hot when you go to bed inside your bag. As the night draws on, however, you get chilled. In those particular times, I sometimes open my zipper down below all the way up to my knees and sleep with the top of the bag zippered below my arms.

That way, my torso and my vital organs are kept warm and my extremities are being ventilated enough to keep cool and sleep comfortably. This happens more than you'd think, especially on a longer trip where you'll encounter more varied elevation. You need to be carrying a bag that will keep you warm on the coolest nights at the highest elevation, but the trail may also dip low enough to make you hot in that warmer rated bag. By ventilating this way, you can make your bag more comfortable over a greater temperature range.

Some sleeping bags can be zipped together, particularly left and right zippers when the bags are made by the same manufacturer. When Todd and I got together, since we were both into the sport before we met, we had about three sleeping bags each. None were the same model, though some were the same make. We got enough to make a warm-weather combination and a cold one. The only trouble was, someone had to sleep with a hood *under* his or her head, where it belonged, and the other, directly *over* his or her face. We took turns.

Zipped-together sleeping bags create more space and, because of it, are often colder. Then you have the other person's movements, besides your own, making bellows that push out the warm inside air and let in the cold air. It's also difficult to tuck the bag around your neck as a collar to keep heat in if your bag mate is sleeping on his or her side with his or her back toward you. (Pet peeves!)

We put up with these inconveniences for seven years until our daughter, Sierra, was born. I felt like we were old married folk when we zipped them separately for the first time. No more legs

wrapped around each other. Todd used to let me put my cold hiney cheeks on his warm belly, to warm me up. Now that was love! It got too difficult to nurse a baby on the inside in a zipped-together bag. Her head was much lower than ours and it would have gotten covered with the bag, preventing her from breathing. It was a hard step to take when we made the separate-bag switchover. Parenthood!

As big as two zipped-together bags feel, they really are too small for three, except in an emergency. We spent a night like that with our buddy, DJ, as a bag mate. We were up on top of 14,500-foot Mount Whitney in the High Sierra. Some climbers got stranded without any overnight gear whatsoever. We were sleeping in the stone storm shelter on the summit built years ago for weather observation. That night, the weather was very cold and blustery. We gave the climbers all of our extra clothing, space blankets, ground cloths, and pack covers to put around them, for they were still shivering dangerously. We then made the ultimate sacrifice and gave up a bag. DJ, Todd, and I got in together. When one needed to turn, we all had to turn the same way. It was a horrendous night. No one slept, but no one died either.

For seven years, we also swore by closed-cell foam pads as insulation under our sleeping bags. When self-inflating air mattresses hit the market, we weren't tempted to make the switch. Closed-cell foam pads had too many advantages over them. They were lighter and *much* less expensive. They could be unrolled and used for relaxing on any surface—rocks or thorns—without fear of puncturing. For any break longer than 10 minutes, the pad comes out for a relaxing rest. Air mattress owners sit on logs or rocks or the cold, wet ground when they gather round a campfire, for fear of a spark burning a hole in their nylon mattress cover. (The only time they get their pads out is in the safety of their tents.) There are no valves to become faulty on a closed-cell foam pad, no pad repair kit to carry. If you need a piece of foam for a pack strap repair or a cushion for your hipbones or to insulate under your stove in the snow, all you have to do is cut a piece off the bottom of your pad. Other backpacking friends told us that once we tried a self-inflating air mattress it would be difficult to go back to a foam pad. We could prevent that problem. We weren't even going to try.

Then we got a phone call from an air mattress company requesting some survey information on sleeping pads that I had gathered from long-distance hikers. In exchange, we'd be getting three self-inflating air mattresses of our choice free. When I got off the phone, I smiled sheepishly at Todd. I thought, we may be breaking down. There are several varieties of pads that are suitable for backpacking. I began to carry a lightweight air mattress and found it extremely helpful in making breastfeeding on the trail more comfortable, for so much time is spent on your side, which is not the most comfortable position on a closed-cell foam pad.

Todd would not make the switch when we backpack. But *someone* needs to carry a pad that we can sit on at breaks. Plus, all the added weight he must carry now because of our children doesn't enable him to justify more ounces for comfort, instead of necessity. Whenever we go car camping, though, you'd better believe he throws those self-inflating air mattresses in the trunk and not the foam pads.

The choice is yours—more comfort as you sleep or more comfort from a slightly lighter pack. If you are *really* concerned with weight, a closed-cell foam pad is the only way to go. And you needn't have a full-length pad, nor even a three-quarter length for that matter. The only place you really need the cushioning is from your shoulders to your hips (providing you use something else for a pillow), when the weather is mostly mild to moderate. That's all Todd carried on the entire Appalachian Trail. For his next long trip, however, his pad went from his head to his knees. And since then, he glued two pads together to go full length. What will it be next, Todd, an air mattress? He says no. Perhaps when his bones begin to get old. Whatever you choose, make sure you stay away from *open*-cell foam pads. It may have an egg carton design and come with a "waterproof cover." They absorb water like a sponge.

Sleeping Gear Hints and Tips

If the rain stops and the sun comes out during the course of the day, pull out your sleeping bag and tent and let them dry in the sun.

Line your sleeping bag stuff sack with a garbage bag to make it more waterproof, especially if your pack is designed for carrying your bag on the outside.

A good idea for a pillow when you're backpacking is to take your extra clothing and rain gear that is not in use and stuff it into the stuff sack that you carry your clothes in, or your sleeping bag stuff sack. Use a cotton T-shirt or a pile jacket for a pillowcase instead of the sack's coated nylon.

You can boost the efficiency of a sleeping bag by wearing long underwear to bed, by doubling up sleeping bags or by using a liner, by sleeping in a jacket and inside a tent, and by eating and drinking before you go to sleep.

Wearing clothes inside your sleeping bag will not only keep you warmer, it will keep your bag much cleaner and add to the appearance and life of your bag.

You can get a whole lot more warmth out of your bag by fluffing and shaking it before you go to sleep to increase the loft, because the trapped air in the fibers is what is really keeping you warm.

In the cold months of winter, sleep can be greatly improved simply by using two closed-cell foam pads instead of one. For cold-weather sleeping, look for a storm collar in your sleeping bag and a zipper draft flap.

If you find yourself shivering in your sleeping bag as the temperature drops unexpectedly, put on your rain gear to act as a vapor barrier and warm you up.

For on-the-trail repairs of a punctured sleeping bag (especially down), use a piece of ripstop tape from your repair kit or a piece of surgical tape from your first aid kit until you can get home and sew a patch on.

On the trail, stuff your sleeping bag rather than roll it, because rolling compresses the fibers at the same place again and again and will break them apart.

Once in camp, remove your sleeping bag from its sack, gently shake it out so the fill lofts up, and lay it out in the tent.

Your sleeping bag will stay much cleaner for longer periods of time if you wash *yourself* up before climbing into it. Even a quick sponging of cool water will lessen the amount of soil and body oil that will collect on the fabric. Changing out of your "hiking clothes" and into "camp clothes" will also cut back on dirt accumulation. Excessive dirt will eventually make its way into the fill, breaking down its ability to insulate.

After a trip, thoroughly air dry your bag before storing it. Hanging it from a line could stress the baffles and the seams. Lay it flat, by drying it on a hammock or spreading it over several lines.

Never store your bag compressed in its traveling sack, for this breaks down its lofting qualities and compresses the fill. A large sack of uncoated material where it can be loosely stored is best.

When not in use, store your sleeping bag in a burlap bag, not wadded up tightly in its stuff sack. The burlap bags are roomy, breathe well, and are fairly rugged. Cut holes along the top of the bag and string them with cord. Tie the cord ends and hang the bag up. To purchase one, inquire at a feed store.

Once your bag gets extremely soiled, it's time to wash it. Polyester-filled bags are considerably easier to clean than down-filled bags. Never dry clean a synthetic bag, for the chemicals can destroy the fibers. Instead, wash in a machine with a mild soap and warm water. Commercial front loaders are best, for they agitate less than a home washer. If you must wash it at home, set only on a gentle cycle. Hand washing is preferred over top loading, agitated washers, for the amount of agitation can be controlled.

Fill the bath tub or sink with warm water and mild soap and gently squeeze and soak the bag for about half an hour. Once the tub/sink is empty of water, press excess water out of the bag with your hands while it lies flat on the bottom. Gently lift the bag out with both arms underneath for support so the weight does not tear the seams. A synthetic bag can be dried in a large commercial dryer but home drying reduces internal strain. Dry over several lines or on a hammock, out of direct sunlight.

Cleaning a down-filled sleeping bag is a very touchy procedure. Only the largest dry cleaners specializing in cleaning down should be considered if you choose to go that route. They must use Stoddard Solvent instead of standard dry cleaning fluids such as percethylene and perchlorethylene, which will strip the down of its natural oils. After dry cleaning, sleeping bags should be aired for several days to remove any cleaning solvent that may remain in the bag. It can deteriorate the down and be toxic to humans sleeping in it.

For home cleaning, use only a bathtub, never a machine. Use a very mild soap or a soap made especially for cleaning down. Only a minimal amount is recommended and extra care must be applied to make sure the soap is rinsed out completely.

Never twist or rub, but gently massage for 5 to 10 minutes. Once the tub is drained, push softly on the bag. Do not lift or squeeze it. Lift the bag out with the support of a large towel or blanket placed beneath the bag. Use additional towels to gently press out excess water.

Dry the same way as a synthetic bag. Once it is damp dry and not heavy from water, place the bag in a large dryer on very low heat with a pair of clean sneakers or tennis balls to break up the clumps of down.

Before a trip, inflate your air mattress to check for leaks and faulty valves. If you find a hole, repair it with your mattress kit. On the trail, electrical tape or duct tape may work in an emergency.

Store your air mattress deflated between trips. Unroll foam pads or roll loosely in storage and avoid setting heavy and sharp objects on top, which could compress and puncture the foam.

If your foam pad becomes heavily soiled, wash it on the lawn with a mild soap and a sponge or soft cloth. Air dry it thoroughly before storing.

Shelter

You don't *have* to purchase a tent before you can venture out on your first camping trip. A tent is one of the most expensive pieces of equipment you will buy and one of the most important, and you don't want to scrimp when it comes to quality. Equipment like a backpack and a sleeping bag are essential. You *could* get by for

awhile with a tarp—a large one, say 9 by 12 feet, until you can afford to buy a good tent.

I hiked the entire Appalachian Trail with a tarp while supplementing it with the trailside shelters much of the time. Tarps have the special quality of allowing you to feel the night breeze on your face and wake up to animals browsing close by. A bad case of freeze-dried farts is much more tolerable under a tarp than in an enclosed tent. There is no barrier between you and the outdoor world and no sense of security either (for those who need that sense of security). Visits from nighttime animals are a different experience. In your tent, you lay inside the enclosed nylon and net and listen for critters scurrying through the underbrush, on their way to check out the kitchen area and your pack. Zippers fly down and flashlights spotlight the culprits, while you never leave the warmth of your bag except in extreme cases. Under a tarp, it could be a little more interesting.

One night while camping on the Black Forest Trail in upstate Pennsylvania, a skunk paid our campsite a visit. First it circled our tarp. I roused my two companions and alerted them of the potential hazard. No one breathed a word. In a little while, the skunk made its way under our tarp and onto our sleeping bags down by our feet. We whispered very softly, "Get! Get!" It wasn't fazed. It began walking up our bags on our bodies, up one and down the other. No one moved a muscle. Next, we raised our voices to the normal speaking level, "Get going, skunk!" It *totally* ignored us. Soon we were shouting at it, "TAKE OFF, BUDDY!" but it took its good sweet time and left when it felt like it, never harming us with its spray or acting strangely vicious. It was merely inquisitive.

Daddy Longlegs slink across your face and arms when you tarp-it in the woods. Insects could be a major problem in some areas of the country, but with good seasonal timing and good campsite selection, they could be avoided.

Rain storms are interesting under a tarp. Even if it's pitched extremely well, the water causes everything to stretch and loosen, tie-down cords and the tarp itself. Sometimes rain settles in depressions in the tarp and forces the fabric lower and lower until it's lying on your bag and your face. I've spent one or two memorable nights with my arm extended, acting as a center pole, in an attempt to keep the wet nylon off me.

Wind can really get underneath a tarp and billow it out like a sail. Open ridges are no place for a tarp, besides the fact that there are no trees to tie it to and suspend it from. Under certain conditions, however, tarps work very well and are more than sufficient shelter. With good trip planning, they will buy you a lot of time while saving for a tent and get you out into the woods far sooner.

An el cheapo tube tent found in Army-Navy surplus stores is another get-by alternative, especially if you plan well and listen to the weather report and only take it out when fair weather is predicted. It will hold up in a light rain, too. My younger brother used one on his first backpacking trip, however, and it poured that night. The way he had it pitched, in a gully, put his sleeping area right in the middle of a freshly made creek. The open ends of the tent enabled the water to move freely through on either side of his bag. Needless to say, the trip was abandoned the next morning and I think he sliced the tube open with a knife and now uses it for a paint throw. (He never did take to the sport of backpacking after that.)

Using your over-the-pack poncho as a shelter to save weight is not the best idea either. How do you go out to the bathroom in a downpour when your rain gear is suspended over your bedroom?

When you do buy a tent, go for one with a separate waterproof rainfly. The one-layer waterproof tents found in some sporting goods departments double as saunas, since they do not allow condensation to evaporate. There are some *very* expensive single-layer tents on the market that are vastly different from the aforementioned. They are extremely lightweight and some are made of a fabric similar to parachute nylon and then coated.

Todd bought one years ago for his 2,100-mile AT hike. After only using it a dozen times, the coating began to peel and lose its waterproofing abilities. By the time he reached New England, rainy nights were a real nightmare. His sleeping bag was stuffed away in its waterproof sack. His pack was inside the tent, covered with its raincover. And he sat in the middle with his rain gear on. Why? He says he didn't know any better. (He was eighteen.) He says he thought all tents performed that way. It *was* supposed to be a good tent. It cost enough.

Wind doubled the fun in this tent. It was supported by two aluminum arched poles, shock corded together, at opposite ends of the tent. One night, the wind blasted it from the side so badly that he had to lie in the middle of the floor and extend both legs and both arms upward to support the four corners and prevent it from collapsing. I believe these grossly expensive tents have been improved. It sounds like there was a lot of room *for* improvement.

A two-layer summer tent with walls consisting mainly of mosquito netting is a joy to have when nights are warm and, perhaps, buggy. You can strip down naked and sleep on top of your bag. The wrap-around floor extends just high enough on the sides to give you the privacy from other campers that you might desire.

Some two-person tents are so tight that you need to be deeply in love with your tent mate. I take that back. You have to be *new* lovers or honeymooners. Many seasoned married folk don't take well to extreme tightness.

As far as a family tent goes, I'd go for one made for one more person than you need—a family of three should buy a four-person tent. Little children, even tiny babies, take up just as much room as an adult, if not more. Many adults know enough to stay on their own side. Both of my children throw their arms to the side when they sleep on their backs. I am always gently picking up their tiny

paws and folding them across their chests to avoid rolling on them and waking them up. And if you have ever spent an extended amount of time with your kids inside your tent in the rain, you would start to care less about its weight and more about your sanity.

We just got a tent that sleeps five. (We have four in our family.) "A monster of a tent," Todd called it when he set it up in the yard to seam-seal it. (He has to carry it.) "We have to find a helluva big camp spot when we set this up." Gone are the days of our little two-person lightweight tents. And he didn't think we needed the 6-foot "cathedral" ceiling. On our very first overnighter with five-month-old baby Bryce, however, it proved to be indispensable. It was a black night. It was raining. And Bryce was crying—long and hard. I had nursed and nursed to the point that I felt like he was going to start sucking blood instead of milk out of me, or at least my brain cells, because it was driving me crazy. Todd finally took him and stood up and jiggled him to sleep in the shelter of our five-person, 6-foot-high tent. We were immediately in love with it.

Over the years, since we've hiked in the open, exposed mountains of the west and through the hellacious mosquito swarms of the lake region, and with children and babies, we now have a difficult time relinquishing our tent for a tarp. We have softened. We have turned toward convenience and comfort. And I think we lost something in the transition. Of course, there is always the option of setting up the tent earlier and moving outdoors to sleep at bedtime if the stars are out and the bugs are in. You can quickly dive into your shelter should the sky cloud over in the night and open up. Our children love the tent. It's a new play space for them. It's one of the best parts of hiking and camping with them. And some newcomers to the sport need its sense of security while they learn to feel comfortable in the outdoors—whatever it takes to get you out there.

Tent Hints and Tips

You can cut down considerably on the weight of a wet tent by shaking the water off before packing it up. Two people grasp the four corners of the tent and bellow it out to the side. Snap it quickly as you move it across in front of you. Repeat a few times until there are no more visible water droplets shaking off the tent.

Your ground cloth will act as a funnel if it extends out further than your tent, directing the rain under the tent floor. Make sure your ground cloth is always tucked in when you set up your tent, or better yet, cut it to fit your floor exactly.

If your tent front slants so that it allows rain to fall directly into your tent when you unzip it to enter, make sure to keep that area free of clothing and sleeping bags. Keep an item like a bandana handy for mopping as you enter and exit.

Inside your tent is no place to cook a meal. Not only does it consume much-needed oxygen and give off condensation in the form of steam, it is extremely hazardous. Place your stove and pot right outside your tent door and cook with the lid on. (Keep your sleeve rolled up if it's pouring and you're not wearing your rain jacket.)

Here's a quick—and dry—method of making camp in the rain: Remove your pack and set it aside with its cover on. Take your tent and spread it out on the chosen spot. To keep it dry, immediately throw your tent fly over the tent body and insert your poles inside your tent body while it's covered with the fly. Stake out the tent, then raise the poles last. Select items that you'll need from your pack for the remainder of the day and toss all of these into your erected tent.

A lightweight tent vestibule can be made of coated ripstop nylon to add that little bit of extra room you can always use on most tents. Where the tent fly overhangs the tent body above the door, velcro should be sewn along the inside edge of the fly. Working with a paper pattern, first construct a triangular piece which will fasten to the velcro edge of the rainfly. Transfer the pattern to the piece of fabric (which you can purchase at most fabric stores). Sear the edges by holding them close to a candle and hem them to prevent unraveling. The triangular point opposite the velcro edge should have a loop sewn onto it which will serve to stake out the vestibule and keep it taut. Velcro can be sewn on both sides of the vestibule so it can be attached on either side of the door, depending on the direction of wind and rain. This vestibule serves as a good place to store muddy boots and wet clothes; it is also a sheltered place to cook in inclement weather.

Most people think it is correct and of course neater to roll up sleeping bags and tents, but it is better to stuff them into their sacks. It is also much faster. When you fold a tent repeatedly, it causes lines of wear to form. The coating will eventually crack and peel if the fabric is stressed at the same creases.

Set up your new tent several times before going on your hike if you are not familiar with the procedure. You'll be especially glad for the experience if a storm is near or darkness is falling.

Use rip-stop tape for on-the-trail repairs until more permanent repairs can be made at home.

Any tent will keep you drier longer after an application of seam sealer. Most tents average ten stitches per inch, which equals thousands of holes that should be sealed. Seal your tent after purchasing it, at least around the rainfly and bathtub seams. Apply the liquid seam sealer to the shinier, coated side of the fabric. Check periodically for peeling, remove it with rubbing alcohol, and replace the sealant. Also check for fraying at stress points.

Spraying lubricant on the zippers and pole sections of your tent will help them to work smoothly in all temperatures.

Carry tent poles and pegs in a separate stuff sack to avoid puncturing the tent fabric.

Direct sunlight is hard on a tent; avoid it if possible. A ground cloth of plastic sheeting will add to your tent's life by giving added protection from punctures by sharp objects.

Keep the tent floor clean of sand and grit while on your trip by brushing with a tiny whisk broom or your hand. After a trip, wipe out the tent floor with a damp sponge.

Keep your tent out of washers and dryers. The coated nylon will quickly peel like sunburned skin. Wash with a garden hose if heavily soiled.

A tent should never be stored while still damp or mildew will grow. Even if it did not rain, condensation from your breathing is enough to cause mildewing. Dry it thoroughly by setting it up on a lawn and letting it air. Hang from suspension points if you must dry it indoors.

Boots

Probably one of the reasons I have such muscular calves is because during most of my hiking career I've worn fairly heavy hiking boots. (The other reason is my genes. My mother had large calves and never did any exercise.) Every pound on your feet is equivalent to five pounds on your back. So the consensus today, with the wonderful array of lightweight boots available, is to go as light as your needs allow. If *all* you are going to do is day hikes with an occasional overnighter or weekend, then the lightweight "glorified sneaker" boot is all that is necessary. It will have all of the running shoe support engineering, be made of quick-drying materials, yet have lug soles for traction.

The rougher your trail gets, the heavier your load becomes, and the colder the conditions, you should move up the scale of boot weight and sturdiness proportionately. If you do a little of everything, and only want one pair of boots, go for a good leather boot. They will offer you the support, protection, and comfort that you will need on those longer, more rugged hikes.

Once you establish your needs, begin to look for a boot in that particular category—lightweight, medium-weight, or heavyweight. Try on different styles from different manufacturers. Some companies lean toward narrow boots, others wide. Bear in mind that whenever you see a seam on a boot, and some lightweights have numerous seams, it is a spot for a potential tear. When you try them on, wear the sock and innersole that you plan on hiking in. A single pair of medium-weight socks is all that is often necessary for most lightweight boots. Medium- to heavyweight boots should be tried on with two pairs of thick socks and your thin liner sock, to insure that they will be large enough for your feet to spread and swell under your load. Your feet usually swell to at least a half size larger than usual.

Try a boot on your largest foot to begin with. (On right-handed folks, it's usually their left foot and vice versa.) Before you lace it, push your foot forward until your toes are against the front. You should be able to easily slide a finger in the space behind your heel. Then tap your heel back and lace it as snugly as you can. You should then be able to wiggle your toes and easily curl them. The boots will feel somewhat uncomfortable around your ankle and across the widest part of your foot until they are broken in.

Make sure they do not fit tightly. When I first began the Appalachian Trail, my leather boots fit me fine, or so I thought. Before long, my toenails turned black. Halfway through the trail, I bought a pair a half size larger. By the time I reached the end in Maine, they too no longer fit. Your feet, it seems to me, would grow bigger and stronger with exercise, just like any other part of your body. There

are muscles in your feet just like everywhere else. And carrying weight must spread them further. Why else do every pregnant woman's feet grow larger as she's carrying her baby in utero, and *stay* that way after she delivers and loses her weight?

I've hiked so many hundreds of miles in tight boots that I now enjoy them roomy—quite roomy. I hate the feel of tight laces across the top of my foot. The leather boots I wore on the Pacific Crest Trail, however, were kept so comfortably loose that the friction on my moving heel wore large holes in my heels—three-layer-deep blisters. After awhile, the skin toughened and my socks just got holes in them but I no longer needed the fabric for protection. I wore holes in the leather heel lining of the boot too. Perhaps they were a little too loose. After my skin healed, though, they felt great.

The uppers on a good leather boot never seem to wear out. I've heard of hikers soling their Limmer's seven times while the uppers stayed just as good as new. (Peter Limmer is famous for making custom-made boots exactly to fit your foot's measurements and have only one seam, in the inside of your boot. His shop is in Intervale, New Hampshire, at the base of the White Mountains.) I've heard of some long-distance AT hikers wearing out three and up to five pairs of lightweight boots by the time they reached Maine. That adds up. Of course, you could just wear sneakers to hike in if you have good sneakers. It can be done. A trail is no place for smooth soles on any footwear, however—sneakers or boots. I hiked with a friend on the Pacific Crest Trail who wore a leather work boot. I suppose it originally came with some very shallow ridges on the sole for traction, but maybe it was smooth from the start. His boots tried to kill him numerous times on the snowy slopes of the High Sierra, by sliding out from under him.

For years Todd wore a single-layer, leather ankle boot with vibram soles. They wore like iron. Since they weren't insulated with another layer of leather, they dried quickly, and the soles gave him the traction he needed on a long rugged trip. They don't make that style anymore and he hasn't found any modern boot to compare to their comfort and cost.

Boots Hints and Tips

Breaking in boots gradually can greatly increase your level of comfort. Breaking in new boots depends on the weight of your boots and what they are made of (stiff leather vs. mostly fabric boots). Lightweight boots require little more than a couple of days walking around town.

Leather boots, on the other hand, could take weeks of gradual wear to break in. A fairly painless method is to start out wearing them a half hour each day with little or no load, and increase until they feel comfortable to wear all day.

To break them in quickly, submerse in warm water for a few seconds. Put them on and walk all day in them. If you condition them immediately after walking them dry, they should suffer little, if any, damage.

I've seen this done twice and both times it worked great. Once was when my boots blew out on the AT and we had to catch a bus into New York City to buy a new pair. The very next day on the trail and for a few days following, it rained steadily. My boots became soaked, but by the time they finally dried, they fit my feet like gloves and never gave me a single blister.

The other time, my hiking partner, Nancy, tried it after buying new boots in town off the Pacific Crest Trail. Since it "never rains in California," she placed them in the motel's bathtub and walked the whole next day in them and got the same results.

Before purchasing boots, always learn which treatment they need. Chrome-tanned leather forms the uppers of most leather hiking boots. For this type of leather, use a silicon/wax conditioner, keeping it away from the sole. Never use oil or grease.

An oil- or vegetable-tanned leather boot will be softer and more flexible. Use an oil base or a grease to condition them, again keeping it away from the sole. Use a high-adhesive sealer for the exposed stitching on your welt.

If boots become wet on a hike, air dry them slowly or put them in the sun. Crumpled newspaper or paper towels can be loosely stuffed inside to absorb internal moisture. Replace the damp paper with dry as needed. Keep boots far away from all sources of heat like radiators, wood stoves, and fires.

Apply wax or grease to boots only after they are completely dry. First remove dirt with a soft brush, for dirt can dry and crack leather and dry out the cement holding the boot together. The inside leather lining can be cleaned/conditioned with saddle soap.

Some suggest a light coating of conditioner in the summer so feet can still "breathe" somewhat, but the boots will still remain reasonably water repellent. Apply it more heavily in wet or snowy conditions.

Make sure you replace your soles before the midsole shows any signs of wear.

Stoves and Fuel

Gone are the days of relying on wood for cooking in the wild. Because of the increased crowds of hikers and campers, firewood is usually depleted at popular campsites. The woods are often dangerously dry in the summer, posing a forest–fire threat. So, carrying a backpacking stove is now more of a necessity than a luxury.

There are two basic kinds of stoves—those using liquid fuels like white gas, unleaded auto gas, kerosene, et cetera, and those using propane/butane canisters. Todd and I will probably be using a Svea white gas stove for the rest of our hiking careers. We each came into our relationship with one, and each of our stoves had 2,100-plus miles on it. Todd had also bought another as a spare when they were on sale. We have used only one of the two older stoves for eight more years and 4,000-plus more miles. (I don't know if we will *ever* get to use the others.) It has never broken down or given us any real trouble in all these years and miles.

It's easy to see we are all for white gas stoves and have never been tempted to try anything else. The propane/butane cartridges go against our conservative side. We'd have a hard time throwing away all of those canisters, when the fuel bottle for a white gas stove is reusable and we only have to carry the amount of fuel we need. It is often impossible to obtain additional canisters in some towns, you never know how much is left in them, and you aren't permitted to mail them in a resupply box.

You don't have to travel internationally to run into trouble periodically finding white gas, or at least in the small amounts that you need. You may not want to purchase a gallon of it, if all you need is a pint to top off your bottle. We've burned unleaded fuel in our Svea stove in a pinch, although it's not recommended by the manufacturer. It makes the stove burn hotter and less efficient, making it sootier. There are liquid gas stoves on the market that are designed for multi-use fuel.

With a little ingenuity, however, we barely ever had to resort to the gas station, even in the wilds of the west. Whenever we got to a campground, the kind campers can drive to, we used to go for a walk with our fuel bottle. We'd cruise the sites, looking for folks who had their two-burner camp stove set up on their picnic table. When we found one, we'd ask if we could buy a cup or two of fuel. No one ever wanted any money for it although we were sure to always offer. One time, I said to Todd before we left on our rounds, "Let's bring our change, just in case someone asks us." We weren't in the habit of bringing it. We would look pretty bad if they said okay and we had no money on us. Sure enough, the fuel donor that day took us up on our offer and wanted $.25!

It's a good idea to ask the salesperson at the camping store to demonstrate lighting the stove you are interested in buying. Then, practice lighting it yourself before taking it out. Under less than ideal conditions, an inexperienced chef could have many problems, resulting in a cold meal. Stoves have individual quirks and need to be handled a certain way. It will take a little time to get to know how it should be treated. Lighting it is one problem. Pressure needs to be built up inside the tank before the fuel can escape through the pin hole and be lit. You can either build pump pressure with the tiny hand pump that comes with the stove, or put gas in the well. Pumping dictates a fine touch and practice or you could have a flare-up or, worse yet, blow up your stove.

We just dump a small amount of fuel in the well and light it. By the time it's burned out, there is usually enough pressure to light the stove. If not, you must wait until the stove cools off before you try again or the gas that you put in the well will turn to vapor.

Always keep your face away from your stove and your pressure relief valve pointed away from you. Place your fuel bottle off to the side when lighting your stove, especially if you neglect to switch the cap from the pour spout to its regular sealed one.

Stove Hints and Tips

A stove that is exposed to a cold wind can take twice as long to cook your meal. In this case, you can take your closed-cell foam pad and make a circle around your stove and pot to shelter it, and clip it closed with a clothespin. (The clothespin doubles as a closure for bags of freeze-dried food that are rehydrating.) Or, you can place water bottles or sacks of food (at a safe distance) or use natural things like rocks or logs to break the wind.

Fill your stove up with fuel after every meal before putting it away so it is full and ready for the next meal and won't run out of fuel halfway through. To insure that you have enough room for expansion and pressure, especially in the cold, fill it only to 80 percent of its capacity.

Be extra careful of spilling sub-freezing fuel on your hands in cold conditions. A pour spout or funnel is necessary.

Regulate your stove's flame so you do not waste fuel when you are doing chores off of the flame like mixing batter or draining water off pasta.

Cut a small section of closed-cell foam pad to use as an insulator under your stove in cold conditions. That same piece can serve as a butt pad for breaks when the ground is cold and damp.

Working your stove can be more of a trial in cold and windy

conditions. Repriming may be necessary, but don't attempt it until your stove has cooled down, for you could easily be burned by the vaporized gas. Fire-starting paste makes your job easier and may be worth carrying in cold conditions.

It takes longer to heat up very cold water or to melt snow. Carrying extra fuel may be required.

A lighter works better than matches for lighting your stove and lasts about three straight months on the trail.

Clothing

Whenever we take our 4-H group of twelve-year-olds out on a backpacking trip, we always go through their packs to see exactly what they are bringing. We always find tons more clothing than is necessary. (Adults aren't any better.) You can definitely save some weight in the backpack by packing less clothing. You don't need much for three of the seasons.

First, there are the clothes on your back. We almost always hike in shorts except for the coldest of days. You want a lot of room in the legs for easy striding. The more you hike, the larger and more muscular your legs will become and the slimmer your hips. Thick cotton shorts will take a long time to dry and may cause some irritation on your upper inner thighs if you have to hike in them while they are wet. (We often swim in our hiking clothes to save the weight of carrying a bathing suit and to give our clothes a much-needed "wash.") A fast-drying fabric for your shorts or at least a thinner cotton may be a better choice.

For your top, use a T-shirt or sleeveless tank top. Todd hikes in a short-sleeved T-shirt and sometimes takes it off altogether when he's very warm. I cannot tolerate short sleeves when it's hot. The heat under my armpits can't evaporate and I'm not fond of a "farmer's tan." Rolling up the short sleeves doesn't work either ... all that bunched-up fabric! I wear a tank top and long-sleeved cotton shirt combination. Then, when I stop on a break and I am chilled, I can easily slip on the warmer shirt.

For your feet, wear thick outer socks made of a wool/nylon or wool/polypropylene blend and a thin inner liner sock of olefin, polypropylene, or silk. One set is for hiking, and you need two to three changes to carry. One set is *always* to be kept dry for sleeping/emergencies. Bring two bandanas—one for wiping sweat and using as a headband, the other for your nose.

In our pack goes only one change of clothing—one T-shirt and one pair of shorts. These are our "in camp/in town" clothes, what we put on after we wash up, what we put on when we must hitchhike into town to resupply, and what we put on to sleep in if we sleep in clothes, to keep our bags cleaner—they should be featherweight. The next day, the old smelly hiking clothes go back on, no matter how dirty or wet from the rain. The spare set would only get dirty or wet within a few hours of hiking and you'd be left with all your clothes dirty and wet.

For warmth, you need a lightweight polypropylene long underwear top and bottom. These go under our rain gear to hike in if it's a really cold hypothermic rain. Next, we bring a wool shirt, wool sweater, or pile jacket. A hat comes along too, except for the hottest days of summer at the lower elevations. We do not bring long pants because the polypro long underwear bottoms and rain pants combination works very well in three seasons. Lycra tights could be substituted for the long underwear, although they are more difficult to get on and off.

When it comes to rain gear, we are not Gore-Tex fans for heavy on-the-trail use. The jackets are often on the heavy side, very costly, and difficult to keep clean during rugged trail use. Gore-Tex does not work well at pressure points, where the "pores" are blocked by pack straps or your entire back when using an internal

frame pack. Coated nylon rain jackets and pants are our favorite.

That's all we take—barely enough to put into your stuff sack to make a decent pillow! Your choice of clothing will vary with the season and the area you are hiking in, but this is a good core wardrobe to start with.

Clothing Hints and Tips

Don't rely on a manufacturer's claim that the fabric or a piece of equipment is waterproof. A pack cover of some sort is necessary to keep the gear inside your pack from getting wet. Use either a coated nylon pack cover specially made for that use, an over-the-pack poncho, or a heavy duty garbage bag with shoulder strap slits cut out.

A balaclava with its long neck protection flap is a great way to add warmth and protection, because a hat is much lighter to carry than an extra shirt or sweater. A balaclava is the best type of hat for warm sleeping, because it covers your neck.

When you first begin to perspire, take off your hat, open your collar, ventilate your wrists, and roll up your sleeves so cool air can go up your arms and cool your armpits. Shirts are good for this reason, for they can help regulate your body temperature. Zippered turtlenecks are excellent choices, but unzippered are very poor at releasing pent-up heat from the neck when participating in active sports such as backpacking and hiking.

Good places to look for inexpensive wool clothing are second-hand stores, Goodwill, and Army-Navy stores.

Using a rain poncho for protection should be avoided when the trail takes you through open and exposed terrain. The poncho will act as a sail and catch the wind. Stick to a two-piece jacket and pants suit under these conditions.

If you want to carry a lightweight pair of pants in the summer to perhaps put on in the evening to ward off insects, bring the thinnest, lightest pants you can find. Avoid jeans. They are too heavy and will take forever to dry if they should become wet.

A good combination for warmth on your lower body is polypropylene long underwear and rain pants, which are extremely lightweight. This combo often makes carrying another pair of pants unnecessary, except in the coldest conditions.

When it is cold out, leave all cotton clothes at home. Cold, wet cotton can kill you.

Water running down your legs often collects and wets your socks and boots. If this annoys you, carry ankle gaiters to keep your socks drier. They can also be worn on an overgrown trail where brushing against the wet branches can also soak your socks.

In the heat, wear clothing that is loose fitting for greater ventilation, and light-colored cotton for its cooling properties. Hats should be light colored too, with the foreign legion style having the best design for sun protection.

Care and Cleaning of Outdoor Clothing

If the manufacturer suggests an alternate cleaning method other than those listed here or a variation, always heed that advice first.

For garments made of down and synthetic fill, follow the same cleaning procedures given for sleeping bags.

Never dry clean a Gore-Tex garment. Dry cleaning solvents will "contaminate" the fabric, making it leak, rather than clean it. Instead, machine or hand wash it. Use a powdered detergent in cold water with no bleach. Rinse on a double rinse cycle and drip dry. Although there are many soaps on the market for cleaning Gore-Tex fabrics, W. L. Gore and Associates does not recommend any of them.

Clean wool garments in a bathtub or a large sink with soap specifically for wool or dishwashing liquid and cold water. Squeeze and massage the garment, instead of scrubbing, to distribute the soap and loosen the dirt. Change rinse water numerous times until it runs clear. Roll the garment in a towel to absorb the excess moisture and lay the garment flat to air dry.

Wash fleece and pile garments in a machine and dry on low heat. To minimize "pilling," which will occur on most garments after extensive wear and repeated washings, wash on the gentle cycle and add a small amount of fabric softener. Brushing the garment with a soft-bristled brush while it dries will also help to reduce pilling.

Gear Hints and Tips

Fold your map to the trail section you will be traveling in for the day and place it in a zip-lock plastic bag. Carry it in your fanny pack for instant waterproof reading.

Wide-mouth nalgene bottles are the best for carrying water. The bottoms, where bacteria can easily grow, are easy to clean. They are easy to fill in a stream or spring compared to bottles with narrow openings. A spoon fits nicely into its wide mouth. They make a great instant pudding container—easy to fill, shake, and clean. They are easier to get partially frozen water out of should the temperature drop and freeze your water. You can also more easily see how much water is left compared to colored bottles or canteens.

Be careful to keep the threads clean on your bottle. Mold and bacteria can easily build up here, especially if you use your bottles for sugary drinks. This can make you sick with dysentery.

Carrying a nylon bladder water bag is a great way to avoid making repeated trips to the spring. You can lay it in the sun and use the warmed water for a shower or use it as a pillow.

Avoid having your flashlight accidently turn on in your stuff-sack by using a rubber band to hold the switch at "off" or by reversing the batteries.

A hiking staff is nice to have on rocky terrain as a third leg for better balance, for reaching over logs or rocks before stepping to warn off an unseen snake, and for flicking debris such as sticks off of the trail and keeping it clear. It can be used as a pack rest prop to lean your backpack against when there are no trees around. It can be used to scare off dogs when you are hiking near a town or on a road, and it comes in handy for retrieving bear-bagged food.

Always store items like toilet paper, your journal, writing paper and stamps, et cetera, in zip-lock plastic bags so they are already waterproofed in your pack in the event of rain.

For backpacking games and fun, take along a frisbee. They're light and can double as a dinner plate or washbowl.

Visors on raincoats usually don't extend out far enough to prevent rain from dripping on your face and wetting your eyeglasses. They also don't turn with one's head. A baseball cap worn under the hood can solve this problem.

You can cut a ground cloth a couple of inches smaller than your tent floor before leaving home to eliminate tucking and save a few ounces on your backpack.

Making Do: Improvising on the Trail

If you ever find yourself on the trail without an important item or piece of gear, the following ideas could make your trip more enjoyable. Or perhaps you don't have the funds to purchase all the equipment you need for a backpacking trip. No need to wait or do without. Make do with these substitutes. You may enjoy some enough to keep them around all the time.

Bandanas can serve many purposes. We usually carry two apiece, with each a different color to help distinguish usage. Here are some ways to use a bandana: Use one as a handkerchief, or as a lightweight bath towel (it will need to be squeezed out several times as you are drying off). A light-colored bandana can be made into a foreign legion–style hat in the sun and heat (it's even better wet). Wear one bandit- or cowboy-style on blustery, cold days. If you leave your balaclava at home, use one to keep your nose warm or to help make breathing easier in dusty conditions. When mosquitoes start buzzing in your ear on tentless nights, try draping a bandana over your face as a head net. On high western trails where summer heat and lingering snow patches are found together, try a snow hat to keep cool: roll up a ball of snow in your bandana and tie it around your head and under your chin. It will keep you comfortably cool while hiking. For women who run out of sanitary napkins, use a folded bandana in place. You can also use one as a bandage.

A worn-out closed-cell foam pad can be recycled by cutting out a small square and placing it under your cooking stove for insulation in cold conditions.

Boot innersoles can be made by tracing your foot onto the pad and cutting it out.

A good "sit upon" can be made by cutting a 12-inch square from the pad and punching a hole in the corner for a loop of cord, so that it can hang on the outside of your pack on a shower-curtain hook. It can easily and quickly be removed to make a warm, soft, dry, clean seat anywhere on the trail. A more effortless seat can be made by punching two holes in the upper corners of the pad, tying a cord through them, and stringing it around your waist. This "butt pad" can be worn while hiking and makes for a quick seat wherever you place your bottom down.

If you get caught in an unexpected snowstorm or accidentally lose your sunglasses or glacier goggles, a makeshift pair can be made out of cardboard. Use cardboard from a cracker box or a guidebook cover or the like, and cut out a form shaped like a pair of goggles. Either cut small slits or punch small holes in the "lenses." The goggles can be held in place by tying rubber bands through holes on either side of the form and looping the bands around your ears.

A pack cover can be made from a large, heavy-duty garbage bag. Cut slits for your shoulder straps and reinforce these cuts with duct tape to prevent further tearing.

A ground cloth can also be made from a garbage bag by simply slitting the two long side creases. A piece of lightweight tarp or a plastic shower curtain would also work.

When temperatures unexpectedly drop at night and you find yourself shivering, slip into your raingear, which will act as a vapor barrier. It works best when it's close to your skin, over polypropylene long underwear. Complete the vapor barrier on your hands and feet by slipping your feet into a coated nylon stuff sack or garbage bag, and using smaller plastic bags for your hands.

To keep your water from freezing in the cold, or to keep it cooler in the summer, slip your water bottle into a sock. Wetting the sock will keep the water even cooler. A more permanent bottle insulator can be made from that old sleeping-bag pad. Trace the bottom of your bottle onto the pad and cut it out; cut another like it for the top. Lay out the length of your bottle onto the pad, including the thickness of the top and bottom discs you've just cut. The width of pad you'll need can be found by wrapping the pad around your bottle. The insulator can be glued together solid and then cut apart later to make it separate into a bottom part and a connected lid. Contact cement works well to glue the joints together. Use tape, rubber bands, or clothes pins as temporary clamps as you let the glue set.

Plastic bread bags or supermarket produce bags make great makeshift gloves while you are hiking, especially if you must keep your hand out of your pocket to hold a hiking stick or an ice axe. Make it a point to always keep a set in your rain jacket pocket.

A good night's sleep is important on a backpacking trip and for some, a pillow is a must. An excellent substitute for that heavy feather pillow is to stuff all of your extra coated nylon (which would need to be stored in your tent anyway) into a stuff sack—rain gear, pack covers, other stuff sacks. A "pillowcase" made of your pile jacket or cotton T-shirt slipped over it finishes it off.

One-liter or two-liter soda/seltzer bottles are great, inexpensive water bottles, and are a valuable replacement for a lost or cracked one on the trail. If you need a larger-capacity water bottle, lots of good bottles can be found in the grocery store containing juice, syrup, or vinegar. Milk jugs are good large-capacity bottles, too, and can be tied onto your pack for in-camp canteen use. Doubled zip-lock bags can serve as a makeshift bladder bag. Pack them in a coated nylon stuff sack for extra protection.

A plastic yogurt container makes a nice drinking cup.

A cake pan or an aluminum pie plate serves both as a deep-dish plate and a lid for your cooking pot.

Don't allow the plastic end caps on your external pack to wear out and fill up with dirt and stones. Replace them with rubber tips made for canes. They won't slip when you set your pack on wet rocks.

If you can't get those tent stakes into the rock-hard earth, or you find yourself short one, use long loops of nylon around rocks or logs to stake out your tent.

Nylon cord can be used to replace broken clevis pins on your pack and also to replace a broken shoelace.

Wire is handy for more durable repairs on pack frames and for boot repairs, such as flapping soles.

Duct tape or electrical tape will work for temporary repairs on punctured down sleeping bags or coats. They will also work as a preventive, moleskinlike bandage on your heels.

Baking soda can be used for much more than baking. It makes a great deodorant, toothpaste, boot powder, and an emergency fire extinguisher.

If the wind blows your wet clothes off your washline, try doubling up your cord and twisting it repeatedly. The cord will hold the clothes tightly if you push corners of the fabric up through the twists.

For candlelight reading in the tent, make sure the candle is placed in a tuna can or a cook-kit lid to prevent accidents. A candle lantern can be cut from a soda can. Cut a 1½-inch strip down the length of the can, leaving it attached at the top. Bend the cut section of the can's side up so it can be hung from the tent's ceiling by a cord or wire strung through a hole punched in the top of the strip.

Food

▲ ▲ ▲ ▲ ▲ ▲ ▲ ▲ ▲

*W*hen I was first planning my AT thru-hike, I built a huge cabinet dehydrator and dried all of the food I thought my partner and I would need on our 2,100-mile journey. We bought nothing from the store but instead made our own cereals, cookies, crackers, et cetera, besides our dinners. We made jerky out of the deer we hunted. We cut hundreds of grapes in half to make our raisins. We spread blankets beneath mulberry tress and shook them for their berries, which we made into fruit leather. We wanted to do it all ourselves. The menu left us wanting—not only variety, but much-needed lunch food. We hadn't realized that on the trail, you could eat breakfast as early as 6:00 A.M. and dinner as late as 8:00 P.M. Were we supposed to hike 14 hours on one lunch? We really needed a half dozen. We were always hungry, especially during the day.

Since I broke my foot on the trail, I had to finish my hike the next year. Our food laid waiting over the winter, in its prepackaged and addressed boxes, ready to go. When we resumed our hike the next year, it was back to those vittles.

Since we never had enough food on the trail, we used to take all our remaining suppers, cook them up, and eat it cold right out of the pot that we carried upright in our packs. It lasted a few days until our next food pickup.

One night, our entire pot of gruel tasted like perfume. Here, over the winter, the soap we had cut apart and triple wrapped leached its fragrance into much of our food. We tried eating it with our noses pinched closed but we still gagged. My partner, in tears, even threw it up. That night I went on a quest to buy food from other hikers.

What we should have done, in retrospect, was throw out the perfumed food, seedy leathers, and rancid granola and cookies (from the oil used in baking), and supplement it with grocery store food. I'm not sure why we didn't make a phone call home to have the unappetizing food removed from our boxes before we paid to have them shipped or why we didn't just chuck it once we received it. I suppose since we put all of that time, energy, and expense into it, we thought we ought to try to eat it. I think it was mostly due to inexperience because we wouldn't have done the same thing today.

When Todd and I got together, I was very sick of dehydrated food. I had thrown out a thirty-gallon trash can full of very dry fruit and didn't want to go that route again. We turned to canned food: shrimp, clams, tuna, oysters, chicken, chipped beef. We planned on two cans a day, one for lunch and one for dinner. We didn't even mind carrying the weight. It tasted too good.

And we went fresh: bread, cheese, green pepper, onion, and tomato sandwiches every day for lunch. Even in the desert the cheese held up fairly well. It melted somewhat during the day but always hardened up just fine in the cool of the night. The tomato we carried in an upright cup in a pocket to prevent it from getting

crushed. The bread we carried in its own specially designed zippered bag that hung on the outside of Todd's pack. Small packets of mayonnaise from the fast-food restaurants completed the sandwich. Sometimes we bought hard salami and pepperoni sticks and a plastic squirt bottle of mustard and I made hors d'oeuvres on crackers.

Then we began testing freeze-dried food for magazine articles and ate like a queen and a king for a trip or two.

Now we've gone full circle and are back to home dehydrating again, on a much smaller scale and with a more selective menu. We also supplement it with grocery store food, are still going with fresh food for lunches, and, if we are fortunate, indulge in a few freeze-dried suppers.

If we've learned anything, the grub on the trail has to taste good. The trail can dish out a lot of hardship to you but your food has to taste good and make you feel good.

One-Pot Meals for the Kitchen Klutz

At every post office drop along the Pacific Crest Trail, my then single husband, Todd, performed the same ritual when he opened up his resupply box. He immediately probed the contents in search of the stuffing mix, for he could not bear the thought of forcing one more spoonful down his throat. Every week it appeared in the menu of his six-month trip and every week it was deposited in the nearest trash can without a second thought. He wasn't alone with these feelings because, to his amusement, he once found unopened packages of stuffing mix *already* in the P.O.'s trash can when he went to lift the lid, left by another hiker.

There's a lot to be said for pretesting your menu before you go out on a hike, especially if that menu must be repeated week after week after week. You don't have to be a gourmet cook either, or even like to spend time in the kitchen, to be able to make satisfying, varied, and delicious trailside dinners.

An unexpected broken foot shortened that journey for Todd, but he returned the next year with a wife and the same weekly menu, including the stuffing mix. It was up to his new bride to make the "stuff" edible.

I added the stuffing mix to a pot of instant mashed potatoes that I had prepared with boiling water and instant milk, according to the box's directions. I threw in some onion flakes while the water heated and some margarine and salt and pepper for flavor. In my pot's lid, I stirred water into a package of instant gravy mix and added a can of chicken. We poured the hot meat and gravy over the potato-stuffing mixture and my Pennsylvania German husband was in heaven.

He was amazed to learn that you could take a basic grocery store item like stuffing mix, add to it, embellish it, and easily turn it into a delicious meal. Most of us are not into making our own bechamel (white) sauce, drying our own ingredients, and taking an hour to get through the eight steps of preparing a home-packaged trailside dinner, including cutting up fresh cloves of garlic into tiny pieces. We want to eat quickly and we'd prefer it to be tasty. And most of us cannot afford a solid dinner menu of tasty freeze-dried dinners. But nobody looks forward to a box of mac and cheese or an instant noodle dinner every single night.

There is another option. The relatively inexperienced backpacking cook can make him- or herself fabulous dinners if he or she keeps a few things in mind and is aware of his or her options.

To begin, let's keep the dinners to one-pot meals. Use a pot with a lid that is deep enough to invert and use as a shallow pan and a food warmer. There are four basic parts that make up a good one-pot meal: 1) your carbohydrate or starch or filler or energy food—pasta, rice, instant potatoes, grains; 2) your protein—meat or fish (or cheese or nuts, if you're vegetarian); 3) a vegetable or two; 4) your sauce/spices. (See the Appendix for dried/powdered foods resources.) Each meal will usually contain one item from each category. You can mix them up to make all the different combinations, but to start, stick to the tried-and-true combos listed below until you have more experience and feel more creatively daring. The items followed by an asterisk are commonly available at health food stores.

Group 1: Starches/Carbohydrates

noodles—spinach, egg, whole wheat*, et cetera

macaroni—whole wheat*, egg

potatoes—instant mashed, hash browns, sliced au gratin, et cetera

rice—instant brown* or white

bulgur—(parboiled cracked wheat)*

Group 2: Protein

canned meats—chicken, turkey, ham, dried beef, smoked fish
canned fish—clams, tuna, salmon, crab
hard salami/pepperoni
smoked sausage
freeze-dried meats (bought in bulk or individual packs)
home-dried meats and fish
cheese—grated parmesan, hard cheddar, et cetera
toasted ground sesame seeds
nut butters—peanut, almond, cashew
bean spreads—canned bean dip, instant hummus*, et cetera

Group 3: Vegetables

freeze-dried (bought in individual packs or #10 cans)
home-dried
mushrooms (oriental food store)
dried vegetable flakes—onions, celery, mixed, et cetera (grocery store—spice section)
dried corn (grocery store)
fresh—carrots, onions, cucumbers

Group 4: Sauces/Seasonings

commercial mixes—gravies, sour cream sauce, sweet and sour sauce, stroganoff, cheese, teriyaki sauces, spaghetti sauce
powdered soup mixes
bouillon cubes
onion and garlic powder
salt and pepper
curry and cumin, et cetera
dried herbs—Italian seasoning, poultry seasoning, et cetera

Here's a sample of winning combinations:

- clams, thin spaghetti, instant milk, garlic powder
- instant potatoes, instant milk, meat, gravy mix, and onion flakes
- rice, ham or chicken, dried pineapple, sweet and sour sauce mix

- potatoes au gratin, tuna, freeze-dried green beans, cheese sauce
- rice, chicken, instant cream of chicken soup, oriental mushrooms (optional), dried onion flakes
- noodles, sliced smoked sausage, freeze-dried peas, sour cream mix, parmesan cheese
- spaghetti, can of tomato paste, spaghetti sauce mix, parmesan cheese
- macaroni and cheese, tuna, instant milk, oriental mushrooms (optional)

After you have made your selections and determined your menu, shop for the ingredients. The packages will inform you of how many servings each contains. Use this information to figure out how much to buy for the duration of the trip. Estimate two to three cups of cooked supper per person per meal, depending on your appetite.

You have a few options on how to combine and package your dinners. Some hikers like their premeasured ingredients in individual bags, and all of these contained in one big bag for each meal with explicit instructions written on it. This method takes all of the guesswork out of cooking once on the trail. All kinks in a dish could be worked out at home where adjustments could be made. However, this method leaves little room for creativity and little margin for error, and entails much more time in the kitchen pretesting amounts, labeling, and packaging.

Todd's hiking partner made all of his curry dishes inedible by overdosing on the amount of curry that he added. Even though it was home tested, he grew to hate the excess on the trail but could not get it out once it was mixed in. Another scenario could be if you mistakenly add too much water to your cream sauce and only have the allotted half cup of milk powder. Your sauce will be soupy and you won't have any extra ingredients to alter it.

I am more comfortable having at least some ingredients that occur in a variety of recipes (instant milk, dried onions, et cetera) in bulk form in my food bag, so I can add and adjust them as needed. I personally estimate all my ingredients and determine the amount of supper I will make at the end of each individual day. How much you want to measure and determine before you leave and how much you want to leave for the trail largely depends on your cooking experience and your personal style.

If you choose to prepackage and measure most or all of your dinners, you should study each ingredient's cooking procedure to determine which ingredients can be combined in a bag and cooked together, and the order of preparation. You can compromise if your noodles call for eight minutes to cook and your freeze-dried beans need to soak for five. Pack them together in a bag and cook until the noodles are almost done, adding your meat or fish and sauce/instant soup just before the end. If your sauce needs to cook or thicken separately, make it in your lid either after your meal is finished cooking or somewhere in between (when your noodles are resting and absorbing a tad more water), and heat it up at the end if need be. Once your order of preparation, amounts, and cooking time are determined, write the instructions with a waterproof marker on freezer tape that is attached to your zip-lock food bags.

Here are a couple of tips to remember if your one-pot meal needs help. Onion powder adds good flavor to nearly any dish. Don't be afraid to be generous with it. (This is not onion salt. Salt separately. You want control over it.) Dabs of margarine enhance every supper and add needed calories and fat. Keep extra instant milk powder on hand to make creamy stew/soup even creamier, besides adding calcium. And if all else fails, and your palate so desires, Tabasco sauce can cover up nearly any dish's faults.

Beyond Gorp: The Search for the Perfect Trail Munchie

I'm going to do something here that your mom rallied against when you were little. I'm going to sing the praises of between-meal snacks. Not only that, but I'm also going to convince you to scarf them down like there's no tomorrow.

You see, when you're on the trail, you eat irregularly, and your hunger overwhelms anything that three meals a day can handle. Maintaining your primary meals helps hold the framework of your food intake together, but snacks provide the real shock absorbers for those unpredictable energy needs that demanding terrain and conditions require.

Basically you should snack almost every time you take a break from hiking. And when you pause to nibble, you should have a variety of snacks to rely on. The following list offers what Todd and I consider to be the best trail snacks out there. Happy munching.

Gorp

The name of this infamous trail snack originally meant "good old raisins and peanuts." It has evolved to include all sorts of exotic nuts, dried fruits, seeds, and candies mixed together into a high-energy snack food rich in proteins, fats, and calories. Because you can eat gorp hand over fist, you can pull out a bag even as you hike and refuel as you go.

You can buy bulk or prepackaged trail mixes, some carrying themes like "Tropical" this and "Safari" that. It's basically gorp, though, and you can easily make a better batch yourself. Classic gorp consisted simply of equal parts of raisins, peanuts, and M&Ms.

Today, even purists liven the foundation up with any of a number of tasty nuggets: nuts, dried fruits, sunflower or pumpkin seeds, shredded coconut, carob chips, chocolate chips (semisweet chips resist melting), and banana chips. Use your imagination.

It may seem like you could never get enough of this tasty and favorite snack. I always looked for more when I was on the Appalachian Trail. Part of the reason was because my two younger brothers used to dip into my supply boxes that lined the rec room shelves when they shot pool after school. My gorp bags were always skimpy when I received them—if they even existed.

Believe it or not, you could go the other way. I once met two AT thru-hikers who had read before they left on their hike that you can't get enough gorp on the trail. So to every town stop they shipped their general food box and a box of equal size and weight containing eight gallons of gorp. This was to be consumed in only a week's time—*every* week, for five or six months. They grew tired of it very shortly and began giving seven gallons of it away at every resupply point. What a huge mistake they made. It was very good gorp, too, and expensive, with lots of cashews in it!

Bread

John Muir prepared for a hike by tossing a loaf of bread and a pound of tea into an old sack. That sounds spartan to many hikers, but it doesn't discount the real pleasure that bread can give.

Logan bread, for instance, is a delicious, dense, chewy bread that's high in calories and almost impervious to spoilage. For an extensive collection of trail bread recipes, consult *Gorp, Glop, and Glue Stew* by Yvonne Prater and Ruth Dyar Mendenhall (The Mountaineers Books, 1982).

If you can't or don't want to bake, search the grocery store for the heaviest, densest bread you can find. You should be able to find hearty seven-grain bread in health food stores.

Candy

Consuming chocolate may be a cardinal sin, but hikers can't seem to keep away from it, and several candy bar manufacturers have created the perfect loophole. They've tucked just enough peanuts inside to withstand legal scrutiny. There's nutrition in there, somewhere, and they're number one with hikers.

If you're not too cavalier, health food stores carry more nutritional candy bars. But if you want to get really serious about candy, try my recipe:

large chunk carob
raisins
nuts
seeds
crispy rice cereal (optional)

Melt down carob in a double boiler. Stir in lots of raisins, nuts, and seeds. Place in a shallow baking pan, spread smooth, and place in the freezer to set. After only a few minutes, take it out to score it so it will break into chunk-size pieces when it hardens. It tastes much like a commercial candy bar, but is better for you and less expensive. The rice cereal adds some crunch.

Cookies

Ah, cookies. There's nothing like them on the trail. If not too sweet, they can double as a decent wake-me-up-now breakfast. I've searched trailfood recipe books and seen this recipe over and over. A chewy cookie like this one travels better than a dry, crumbly one.

Peanut Butter Super Cookies
1 cup margarine
1 cup chunky peanut butter

1¾ cups brown sugar
2 beaten eggs
¼ teaspoon vanilla
2 cups whole wheat flour
2 teaspoons baking powder
2 cups granola or oatmeal, or 1 cup each raisins and chopped
*   peanuts*

Cream together margarine and peanut butter. Add sugar, eggs, and vanilla. Mix in flour and baking powder. Add granola or oatmeal, or raisins and peanuts. Drop huge spoonfuls onto a greased cookie sheet, and flatten with a fork. Bake 10 minutes at 350°. Remove from the oven when the cookies are still on the chewy, undone side. This recipe makes eighteen huge cookies.

There are many popular grocery store brands of soft cookies, and several oatmeal varieties are fairly nutritious. Ginger cookies—the hard, indestructible, and spicy kind—become heavenly treats with cream cheese spread on top. Cream cheese will keep for two to three days if stored in an airtight plastic container.

Fresh Produce

We're sold on the virtues of fresh foods, and we never leave town without buying a hefty onion for sandwiches. We particularly love green peppers because of their light weight. Tomatoes do well if cut and eaten in one sitting. Sprouting superlight alfalfa in water bottles capped with cheesecloth adds variety and spruces up your sandwich. Fresh peaches, apples, and bananas are also great treats, but you'll want to eat them early in your hike before they spoil and to get rid of the weight.

Jerky

Every convenience store sells some variation on the jerky theme, but most commercial brands are laced with a lot of chemical additives. Making jerky at home provides a healthy alternative and is really simpler and less expensive than you might think.

Flank beefsteak works well. You'll find slicing easiest when the meat is partially frozen. Cut off all visible fat. Cut sliced, fillet-style layers into thin strips across the grain. Cut these strips as thinly as possible and of uniform thickness for even drying. If you wish to marinate, place strips in a shallow glass baking dish, cover with your marinade, and cool in the fridge overnight. The next morning, drain well and place the strips in your dehydrator; or, if you don't have a dehydrator, lay them close together—but not touching—on cookie cooling racks. If you have a gas oven, the pilot light will work fine for the drying process, or turn your electric stove on its lowest setting. Keep the oven door propped open for air circulation. Drying will take anywhere from 12 to 48 hours. You know your jerky is done when you can snap the strips in half by bending them.

I don't like my jerky too dry, so I keep it in the freezer until it's ready to be used or mailed. The drier the jerky, the longer it will keep unrefrigerated.

Peanut Butter, Crackers, and Cheese

I know of many a long-distance hiker who depends on peanut butter as a snacking mainstay. Carry it in a plastic container because squeeze tubes inevitably leak. Monterey jack cheese keeps surprisingly well on the trail.

Popcorn

Popcorn? Absolutely. We made popcorn almost every night for three months while hiking the Cascades and never got tired of it. That's saying a lot. Best of all, even the worst trail cook can make it. It's lightweight, and our seasoning mix gives it a gourmet panache. We added salt, onion/garlic powder, a sprinkle of cayenne pepper, dehydrated butter (found in the supermarket "spice" section), and parmesan cheese.

Snack Bars

Grocery store granola bars have metamorphosed into candy, and you'll want to stay away from most of them. Some of the better varieties contain oats high in complex carbohydrates for sustained energy, instead of only quick-fix, simple sugars. They're also tough and durable; they seem to last forever and will give your jaws a good workout.

Health food stores offer some useful alternatives, though most are very expensive.

Movable Feasts: Camping Breads

It doesn't take many days of trail hiking, where you eat pot after endless pot of soft, mushy, mixed-together gruels, before you begin to crave something with more substance, something that needs to be chewed, not gummed, and also fills up that ever-empty pit of a stomach. The answer is bread.

Just the thought of carrying bread, to some backpackers, is impractical and close to impossible, let alone making it fresh in the wild. But only on those occasions when a superheavy pack of extra gear and extended supplies force you to weigh every ounce should you think twice about this forgotten staple.

Homemade "quick" breads using baking soda or baking powder as a leavening, instead of finicky and time-consuming yeast, are indeed very quick, easy, and virtually idiot-proof. If you can read down a list of ingredients and combine them in a bowl or two, you are capable of making delicious, nutritious camping bread.

To carry along make-at-home breads is the easiest way to keep in-camp cooking simple. Merely take the well-wrapped bundle and slice or tear hunks off at your meal or when the mood strikes. At home, where you're not competing with wind, fatigue, lack of work space, or impending darkness, may be your best place to start. A few tips can help the end result be more successful.

If possible, ingredients should be at room temperature or a little warmer before starting. This prevents raw centers and dark crusts, because cold batter heats unevenly in the oven. (If it can't be prevented, cover with foil for the remaining time needed to bake the center.) Mix *only* to moisten ingredients so no pools of powder lie in the bottom of the bowl. Unmixed "flavor morsels" taste disgustingly bitter and salty and will ruin your mouthful. But overbeating will destroy the rising gas in the soda or powder and your bread will turn into a "brick." When an inserted toothpick comes out clean with no gooey batter on it and the sides of the loaf shrink away from the pan, the bread is done.

Quick-bread recipes usually call for a higher fat content, adding welcome calories, but also making the bread firm, solid, and moist, so it won't crumble in your pack, even after days of jostling. We carry our bread in an additional, strapped-on, outside pocket, or place it in the very top of our packs.

The wonderful combination of caraway seeds and raisins make this quick bread recipe my all-time favorite.

Pioneer Bread

½ cup butter or margarine
½ cup honey
3 eggs
1 cup buttermilk
2 cups whole wheat flour
2 cups unbleached white flour
1 teaspoon baking soda
1 teaspoon salt
1 cup raisins
2 tablespoons caraway seeds

Combine butter, honey, and eggs in a bowl. Then add buttermilk. Separately, combine flours and baking soda. Then add salt, raisins, and caraway seeds. Combine both bowls. Place in a greased loaf pan. Bake at 375° for 50 to 60 minutes or until done. My loaf always seems to take much longer. (A good substitute for buttermilk is to add 1 tablespoon vinegar to your 1 cup of milk and let stand for a moment.)

On-the-trail bread-making need not be mysterious or complicated. One company has developed a cook-pot accessory called BakePacker that enables anyone who can mix water and powder

and boil water to make steaming, fresh, delicious bread in the wilds. (See the Appendix for ordering information.) It is a pot insert consisting of an aluminum grid that functions as a heat exchange. Instant bread and muffin mixes that are purchased at the grocery store are mixed and baked in a plastic bag, spread over the grid and boiling water while still inside the bag, and produce/create baked goodies in a matter of minutes. Our favorite was a corn bread that was a welcome addition to our evening meal.

Bannock is an old-timer's flat bread that closely resembles biscuits but is usually fried in a skillet. Both bannock and biscuits, however tasty, take more time and skill than most backpackers have. Consider dumplings as an easier and tasty alternative. Dumplings are basically biscuits cooked by steam that are plopped on top of your nearly cooked stew or hearty soup and left undisturbed with a lid on for 15 to 20 minutes while they double in size.

The dumpling mix can be packaged in a zip-lock bag at home so all you have to do is add water, mix, and drop golf-ball-size dollops on top of your meal. Either use biscuit mix, following the directions from the manufacturer, or:

Whole Wheat Biscuit Mix for Dumplings

1 cup white flour
1 cup whole wheat flour
2 teaspoons baking powder
1 teaspoon salt
2 tablespoons shortening or oil
¼ cup powdered milk

Combine at home in a zip-lock bag. In camp, add 3 tablespoons water per ½ cup biscuit mix and mix well. Spoon into boiling stew or soup. Cook 10 minutes uncovered and 10 minutes covered. From *The New Healthy Trail Food Book* by Dorcas Miller (Globe Pequot Press, 1980), no longer in print (pages 33 and 52).

Another simple way to include hot, tasty bread in your trailside meal is to bring a good, solid, store-bought loaf along. Butter both sides of a slice with margarine, sprinkle with garlic powder and a little oregano, and fry in your lid. It's superb with trail spaghetti and lasagna. For breakfast, sprinkle cinnamon and brown sugar on your margarine bread for a treat much like a warm sticky bun. It's called "Todd's Famous Fried Bread," after my husband, who made it for me on our first date, on the trail, while still in his sleeping bag. It may very well have been the deciding factor. Never underestimate the power and goodness of "Camping Breads"!

Rescuing Your Food

There's a long-held notion in the world of backpacking that anything you cook in the backcountry tastes great. Proponents of said theory hold that after sucking trail dust all day and washing it down with iodine-flavored water, even tree bark is savory.

I confess that I don't count myself among those people. I actually want to enjoy my meals, and end the day's repast with a pleasing sigh. You needn't be a culinary genius to rescue bland and tasteless backcountry meals. It merely takes a bit of imagination, basic spices from home, and a willingness to try something new. Trust me on this and you'll be the envy of your drooling campmates.

Want to add Italian flair to your tomato-based dinner? Add dried basil and oregano, which can be mixed and carried in the same container. Lend an Indian flavor to your chicken and rice (or any bland chicken dish) by tossing in some curry and a few raisins from your gorp. Even a rich dish can benefit from curry and raisins. And cumin will make a bean dish more "Mexican."

Two seasonings you shouldn't leave home without are garlic powder and onion powder, because they can enhance nearly every meal. Go lightly on the garlic, though, unless you're exceptionally fond of it and want to hike alone. (If you're trying to limit salt intake for health reasons, avoid garlic and onion salts.) Dehydrated garlic and onion flakes supply even more flavor, but must be added while you're cooking so they can rehydrate. Dried parsley lacks a strong flavor and isn't worth the space it takes up in your pack. Cinnamon and nutmeg are easy to carry and can make bland oatmeal more palatable. Banana chips, chopped dates, raisins and other dried fruits are also easy additions to oatmeal.

Bouillon is another good flavor-enhancer for chicken or beef dishes, but it, too, often contains extra salt. Individually wrapped bouillon cubes stay moisture-free longer than granules, which tend to clump and harden. Borvil, a dark, sweet-smelling liquid, has a delicious beefy taste and can be used in place of bouillon. It's found in larger, well-stocked grocery stores or gourmet stores.

For more basic food rescue, add instant tomato or cheddar cheese powder. (See the Appendix for dried foods resources.) Grated parmesan and romano cheeses also travel well. Instant soups like cream of mushroom and cream of chicken are also good flavorers, and come in easy-to-carry envelopes. Dried butter-flavored bits usually found in the spice section of the grocery store, squeezable margarine, or a stick of margarine kept in a wide-mouth water bottle are lightweight flavor enhancers. The extra fat is essential on a long trip because body fat reserves are used up.

Don't neglect other seasonings that might seem a bit "exotic."

Dried mushrooms, bacon bits, flavored croutons, and sesame, poppy, and sunflower seeds are all easy to pack and light in weight.

So you've got flavor, but does your meal still have the consistency of gruel? Watery stews aren't nearly as filling and hearty as those with a nice thick gravy. If you've already added enough spices, then stick with milk, tomato, and cheese powders to thicken things up. Or you can make gravy by simply adding a small amount of flour to a little cold water in your cup, then stirring until the flour dissolves; 1½ tablespoons of flour will effectively thicken 1 cup of liquid. A little cornstarch or arrowroot powder works just as well.

If you choose, you can take along packets of commercial gravy mixes found in the grocery store. Merely follow the directions on the envelope, and add water to the dry mix little by little. Dump the envelope's contents into a pot of water or soup and you'll end up with undissolved gravy chunks that will raise the hair on the back of your neck.

If you want to avoid the additives in commercial gravy and sauce mixes, either make your own, or carry instant potato flakes or instant baby cereal in a sealed bag. The tiny freeze-dried crystals thicken and bulk up your meal in seconds and can be added right to the pot without premixing. Baby cereals are a wonderful source of additive-free grains and come in a variety of choices, including one that's very bulky and high in protein. I learned this trick while backpacking with my six-month-old daughter. I desperately needed to thicken supper, and her cereal was all I had. It worked better and faster than anything else I've tried.

If you're feeling adventurous, mix up your own white sauce at home:

1 tablespoon dried butter morsels
1½ tablespoons flour
2 tablespoons dry milk

Label and put in a bag with directions, "Add 1 cup of water." It makes a medium-thick sauce and serves three.

I have some friends who try to stretch prepackaged meals, which in my view is a good way to capture the oh-so-delicious flavor of hospital fare. My friends add a package of ramen noodles to something like a prefab noodle dinner to "make it go further." The result is always lots of noodles and little, if any, taste. What they should do is increase the seasoning along with the bulk. If someone runs out of food and you have to stretch a prepackaged dinner, look at the package, see what herbs and spices the manufacturer added, then add more of the same seasonings. If it's a creamy dish, add instant milk and some additional water. Always pack more instant milk than you'll need for cereal and instant puddings; besides making a dish creamier, milk adds protein and calcium.

I carry a small stuff sack as a spice bag with a GI can opener attached to the pullcord. All the herbs and spices are stored in small, plastic food grade containers. Use transparent containers so that you can see what's inside, or label your containers. Bouillon cubes should be carried in their own small, sealed plastic bag since they melt in the heat. Package all powders at home in individual bags, enclosing directions for mixing if necessary.

One more small bit of advice: If all the herbs, powders, and sauces fail, cayenne (red) pepper can be used as a last resort. It won't give you much variety, but I guarantee your dinner won't be bland.

Food for the Long Haul: An exclusive study of long-distance hiker eating habits

If you're anywhere near the Appalachian Trail during the thru-hiker season, you're likely to encounter at least one backpacker sporting a "Please Feed the Hiker" T-shirt like a billboard. Zoos may admonish you to keep food to yourself, but you'll find a generous handout to a ravenous trail animal can be a saving grace.

Hunger rides herd on everyone out there, especially long-distance hikers. No matter how much mac-and-cheese you pack, there's never enough. One look at the thin, haggard bodies of thru-hikers approaching Mount Katahdin tells the story.

Nor do hikers get the proper nutrition their bodies need, which over the course of a long trip can defeat an otherwise sound effort.

Karen Lutz, a Pennsylvania State University student from Pittsburgh, encountered this continuous hunger while hiking from Georgia to Maine in 1979 and decided to devote her master's thesis to it. She focused on three areas: the changes in a hiker's body composition over a long hike; the nutritive value of a typical long-distance hiker's diet; and the number of calories expended during such a trip. The results of her study can help all hikers better plan their menus.

To catch the AT thru-hikers early in their journeys, she set up shop in April at Amicalola Falls Park, Georgia, along the approach trail leading to Springer Mountain, where most thru-hikers begin the long march north. She weighed them, measured them, and determined their body fat. She queried them on their diets, and calculated the calories, protein, calcium, iron, thiamine, and vitamins A and C. Then she wished them well and sent them on their way.

She repeated the examinations midway between Georgia and Maine and then in Baxter State Park, Maine, the northern terminus of the AT.

The hikers ranged in age from twenty-four to thirty-three years old. All weighed less when they finished than when they began—an average of twenty pounds less. The smallest weight loss was eight pounds; the largest, thirty-two.

All hikers lost body fat but the men lost an average of seven pounds of *lean* body weight and muscle tissue as well, something that's supposed to happen only when the body is under extreme physical stress. Lutz discovered this to be the norm on the trail, however. The one woman in the study was the only hiker who did not burn up lean body weight, and she even gained muscle mass. (Women's bodies have a higher ratio of fat to muscle than men, and therefore a greater buffer of fat to burn before drawing on muscle tissue.)

Lutz discovered that most hikers ate more than 5,000 calories a day, but not a single hiker reached the 6,000-calorie level needed to maintain his or her normal body weight. The dilemma is an interesting one. The more food you carry, the greater the pack weight and the more energy required to carry it. The more energy you need, the more you eat. In other words, weight loss is to be expected.

Of the nutritional failings, she discovered calcium deficiencies to be the greatest. This is supported by long-distance hikers' frequent complaints of muscle cramps, which calcium generally helps prevent. The hikers suffered a deficiency of vitamin A, found in the dark leafy greens and orange veggies that are often difficult for hikers to come by. Many hikers have reported extreme sensitivity to light while driving at night after their trip—a good indication of vitamin A deficiency.

For more vitamin A, eat dried apricots and other fruits on a regular basis. Dates, raisins, and figs aren't extremely high in calcium, but a steady supply throughout the trip can increase calcium and vitamin A levels. You can further benefit from learning to identify wild edibles and greens and incorporating them into the evening stew.

Adding powdered milk to various dishes, especially soups and stews at supper (make a white cream sauce), or as a beverage, can also boost calcium intake. Cheese provides an excellent source of protein and calcium and can be carried easily for days. Oil-packed sardines, almonds, and filberts are also good sources of calcium.

Thiamin, a B vitamin, was also lacking significantly, which is no surprise, since some of a long-distance hiker's favorite foods, processed rices, pastas, and instant oatmeal, have little or no thiamine content. Hard physical work and stress, two factors abundant on long journeys, call for increased thiamine intake. Increased consumption of sugars and starches (carbohydrates), which Lutz observed as the miles ticked off, creates an even stronger need for thiamine, which oxidizes carbohydrates and converts them to energy.

To boost the vitamin B content in your hiking diet, try carrying rolled, unprocessed oats instead of instant. Soak them overnight in a pot of water and they'll cook like instant in the morning. Choose whole grain, instead of processed, bread and crackers. Since the B vitamins are more potent if used together, it's wise to increase intake of all of them at once. Nutritional brewer's yeast, found in health food stores, is an excellent source of these vitamins and can be carried in a small plastic bag and tossed into the evening meal.

Forays into town grocery stores and restaurants along the way let hikers make up for dietary problems on the trail. And an interesting thing happens when you finally hit the streets. You crave exactly what your body needs most. A typical thru-hiking nomad will inhale a half-gallon of ice cream, milk, or yogurt immediately, which attacks the calcium deficiency. Then he or she heads to the nearest salad bar, which provides the greens needed for vitamin A.

Horror stories aside, if you anticipate your dietary needs and stick to a good food program, you can avoid severe weight loss. I learned this good lesson the hard way.

Envisioning the weight loss of twenty to sixty pounds that I had seen on other AT thru-hikers, I ordered a bridesmaid dress for my sister's wedding which was scheduled to immediately follow my completion of the AT. I specified a smaller size than I ordinarily

wear. To my chagrin, I lost a mere five pounds and had to go on a
crash diet to get into the dress.

A good diet can only help you feel better and stronger on the
trail. And sometimes that's all that's necessary to keep going.

Dehydrated Food

You don't have to like to cook or even know how to make a dehydrator for home-drying of foods to be worthwhile. Today's
counter-top models make it easy to dry already prepared meals
like your leftover hearty soups, stews, and casseroles. (See the Appendix for home dehydrator resources.) If you don't cook, you can
purchase cans of beef stew and soups and the like and dry them
right out of the can for excellent and quick trail meals. What's the
reason? A solid sheet sits on top of the screens and will dry almost
any creamy or semiliquid food, including puddings, yogurt, and ice
cream. We took a one-and-a-half-pound can of beef stew and sub-
stantially reduced its weight to five ounces by drying it. A nine-
teen-ounce can of clam chowder was reduced to four ounces.
Cooking time took 10 to 15 minutes without soaking and could
have been less had we presoaked.

What's New in Dehydrators

Todd and I have used two different major manufacturers' counter-
top dehydrators and are very pleased with both. They are *not*
batch-type dehydrators—that is, a dehydrator that is loaded and
not emptied of its contents until all the food in it is sufficiently
dried. (Batch-type dehydrators use more electricity and are not as
efficient.) These particular dehydrators are round, with stackable
trays. Fan-forced warm air rises through the trays of wet food and
exits out the top of the dehydrator with the moisture. You take off
the trays of food from the bottom as they dry and add trays of
fresh food to the top. This way, you never mix the moisture of the
wetter food with the food that is already partially dried. Trays are
not rotated as in the batch-type dehydrators.

A real treat to make and to eat is fruit-flavored yogurt roll-ups.
You can do this with a dehydrator that has solid plastic sheets
with a lip that enables you to dry semiliquid foods. The dried yo-

gurt tastes like tangy saltwater taffy. Whenever we dried a batch, it was so delicious it never made it to a hiking trip but was eaten right then—warm. And don't names like "Strawberry Cream Cheese Roll-ups" and "Banana Coconut Cream Roll-ups" set your mouth watering? This high-calcium addition to your trail lunch menu is even more desirable when you consider that many hikers suffer from calcium deficiency.

We've found that a dehydrator with plastic sheets on which to dry your roll-ups is preferable, but you must be able to spread, not pour, a liquid food before you can use them.

One of the best things about drying semiliquids is the chance to eliminate heavy items such as cans of tomato paste for spaghetti sauce on the trail. All I had to do was mix up a batch of my Italian mother's recipe for sauce on the stove, spread it out, and wait for it to dry. I broke up the pieces into chunks and merely added water on the trail and simmered. I actually could not tell the difference between the meal I enjoyed at home and the rehydrated version on the trail. If you don't have a good recipe at home to dry, spaghetti sauce from the grocery store will make a good substitute.

Nearly anything you are having for supper at home you can dry and enjoy on the trail—hearty bean soup, chili, refried beans, et cetera. Experiment. Some meals lend themselves better to drying and rehydrating. Try noodle dishes like tuna casserole or lasagna. (Always sample a rehydrated meal at home before taking it on the trail, just in case something goes wrong with the process.)

A dehydrator with the option of an aluminum jerky press enables you to make your own jerky out of ground meat. Traditionally, home jerkers used flank steak and had to cut away all signs of fat and gristly membrane. It was time-consuming, and, although cheaper than manufactured packaged jerky (about $20 a pound), it was still costly.

With the hand press, you can use extra-lean burger or even turkey burger if you want to avoid beef. And hunters, don't forget to try your ground venison. You merely roll the ground meat into small balls, insert in the press on its reusable plastic liner, press, peel, and lay out on the dehydrator trays to dry. You have your choice of ⅛-inch strips, or thinner double strips on the press' other side. You can also try your hand at making granola bars. Consult the manufacturer's instruction and recipe book.

Of everything these new dehydrators can do, perhaps the

most frequent way we use them is to simply dry the foods we eat on the trail in bulk—cooked brown rice, chicken cubes, apple slices, et cetera. By buying food on sale, and using the overabundance when the garden is producing madly, we save considerable amounts of money. Look for creative sources of food—a generous neighbor's successful catch from deep-sea fishing; deer from a hunter friend whose family doesn't care for the taste of venison; leftover ham at Easter and turkey at Thanksgiving. We have found that by preparing our trail meals at home with the dehydrator, we have extended the joy of an outing and made the pleasure and excitement last even longer.

Food Hints and Tips

Butter gets rancid in the heat, but it is an important source of fat on an extended backpacking trip when your body's fat reserves are depleted. Carry margarine instead in a tight-lidded plastic container. Add it to your morning oatmeal and supper stews for added calories, taste, and fat.

When going on a backpacking trip for any length of time, always supplement with high-potency vitamin and mineral tablets.

Double-plastic-bag your instant milk powder to avoid punctured bags and spilled powder. Avoid zip-lock bags for packing milk, as the fine granules get caught in the channel and prevent the bag from closing.

Consider oriental food stores and health food stores besides general grocery stores for trail-food menu ideas.

When making a large amount of pasta in a small pot or with less than the recommended amount of water, stir it as infrequently as possible—two or three times—and do not let it soak and it should not come out gummy.

In warm weather, eat the food from your pack that is highest in fat and egg content first, because it will be the first to spoil.

Don't stuff yourself at any meal during the day while you are hiking, because you can easily get indigestion. Instead, eat small amounts often. Do not plan on climbing on an empty stomach. Even if you do not feel hungry, stop for a snack before ascending to give you the extra energy you may need to get up the mountain.

You can carry fresh eggs on a trip even in hot weather if you first submerge the eggs into boiling water for just 5 seconds. They will then keep for a couple of weeks.

Flavored gelatin is a good trail food and a welcome switch from the norm. Mix it up at night when you are boiling water for your dinner or a hot beverage. It will be set in the morning whether you are near a stream to set it in or not. Pour the hot liquid into its own plastic container with a lid and eat it throughout the course of the day.

Wooden spoons are light, have long handles so they don't disappear into the soup pot, and don't get hot when left in the pot. Whoever doesn't carry the wooden spoon should bring a metal tablespoon for those times when supper or your oatmeal sticks fast to the pot and the removal job calls for more than what your scrubbie can provide. Scrape your metal spoon on the bottom of the pot to remove much of the cooked-on food before attempting to scour.

Don't be misled into thinking that drink mixes and gelatin mixes containing NutraSweet are a better idea (if you don't need the calories) because you don't have all the weight of the sugar to carry. Use sparingly if you eat it. We allotted one NutraSweet drink mix and one NutraSweet gelatin mix per day on one trip and that was enough NutraSweet in our bodies to induce diarrhea.

If your overall pack capacity is small, some kinds of food can be compressed to save on space, i.e., bread and cereal can be crushed. We have a hiking friend with bright red hair called "Redman" whom we later nicknamed "Redman Breadman," for he always purchased three loaves of bread upon leaving town and squeezed them into a single bread bag.

You can burn your supper calories up quickly when the evening is a cold one, sending you to bed with your stomach empty and your body cold. Refuel by eating high-caloric food before turning in and take a snack to bed with you, if conditions allow, in case you wake up in the middle of the night starving.

Always use a lid when cooking. It makes the contents heat quicker, keeps them warmer longer, and uses less fuel. If you have stackable pots and are preparing a sauce after you've cooked your main dish, put that pot on top, so the bottom one's rising heat keeps it warm until mealtime.

Menu Ideas

Breakfast

instant oatmeal or other instant hot cereal

homemade or commercial granola

fruit—dried or fresh

hash brown potatoes (with onion powder and cayenne pepper)

fresh eggs (from a foray to town)

dehydrated eggs with spices and herbs

dried sausage

honey, brown sugar

beverages—tea, instant hot cider, coffee, instant egg nog, instant roasted grain coffee substitute, hot chocolate

instant milk—add to cereals and eggs for more protein and calcium

donuts, English muffins, raisin bread (from town)

toaster pastries

breakfast squares, bars, instant drinks

fruit juice—orange and grapefruit

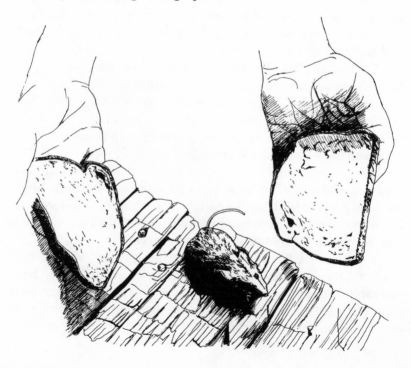

Lunch

bread
crackers
cheese (hard cheese won't melt)
green peppers
onions (long shelf life)
salami, pepperoni
mustard
hard-boiled eggs (cooked in town)
alfalfa sprouts
oranges, apples, et cetera
carrots, cucumbers
sardines
tuna
potted meat—chicken salad, meat spread
popcorn—oil, or package margarine in plastic home sealing
  pouches
candy—licorice
dried or fresh fruit
nuts
sunflower seeds
instant pudding
granola bars
jerky (you can make your own)
gorp—peanuts, raisins, M&Ms, shredded coconut, et cetera
soups
cookies—big bars, hard cookies
trail breads (make ahead and keep for months)
peanut butter—assorted butters
banana chips
fruit leathers
cream cheese and ginger snaps
extra bouillon cubes, gravy mixes, soup mixes when dish
  needs more flavor

Supper

macaroni and cheese/tuna/dried onions/instant milk/mar-
  garine or whole wheat macaroni and cheese sauce
  package

ramen noodles/clams/instant milk/garlic powder/Italian
   seasoning
instant potatoes/milk/dried onion and onion powder/mar-
   garine
add on top—envelope of chicken gravy/canned or dehydrated chicken
whole wheat noodles/tuna/dried mushrooms/cream of mushroom soup/milk
spaghetti mix/can of tomato paste/Italian spices
fried bread with butter, garlic powder, oregano, and basil
dehydrated potato shreds/dehydrated ham/ dried green pep-
   pers/onions/string beans/cheddar cheese—dehydrated
   or sauce mix
instant flavored rice mix/canned or dehydrated meats
chicken/pasta/cream of onion soup mix/sour cream
   mix/almonds/dried peas
packaged hamburger and tuna helper
noodles almondine, romanoff, et cetera
instant cheesecake mix, chocolate mint pies, et cetera
many assorted noodles
textured vegetable protein (TVP) in assorted flavors
spices: chili powder, onion powder (tons), garlic powder,
   Italian seasonings, cinnamon-nutmeg

Preparing for a Hike

▲ ▲ ▲ ▲ ▲ ▲ ▲ ▲ ▲

*D*o you absolutely *need* to get your body in shape before a backpacking trip? That depends on your body. The more body work you do beforehand, the more it will help ease the sore muscles on the trail. There is often little available time for an extensive training program, however. When I was preparing for my first AT journey, the only exercise I could do was walking up and down sixteen flights of stairs twice a day in my Philadelphia apartment house. Part of my incentive came from the fact that twice that year the elevator broke and went crashing down to the basement. As an art student at the time, I had little free time to get in shape. Before other long trips, I began jogging only a few weeks prior to departure. I don't know if it did much—perhaps it built my endurance and stamina up a bit—but I felt foolish going out on the trail without even a token effort.

I live a fairly active life and my muscles are somewhat used to having a pack on my back. I've carried a child to the mailbox a mile away for the last few years. Before having my children, I backpacked often enough to have it barely bother me. The first few times I ever carried a pack (back when I was sixteen), my shoulders absolutely revolted. This is where our backpacking students complain of the pain the most. If you are just beginning, it would be wise to put on a loaded pack while wearing your hiking boots and carry it up and down uneven terrain. Stuff your sleeping bag in loosely and place some heavy objects such as a thick dictionary on top of it. This is the best exercise you could do to prepare. All the running, cycling, swimming, and weight lifting won't do nearly as much as this. Walk to the grocery store, to work, to run your errands. People will look at you strangely (they did at me in downtown Philadelphia) but take no notice. Before we left for a long trip, we never seemed to have the extra time to go on a weekend shakedown trip because we were so busy preparing for the real trip. Do what you can. The more you're using your body and its muscles in your daily life, the less trail pain and discomfort you will experience. If you live a relatively sedate life, be prepared for some pain. Bring along aspirin. If you are overweight or have health problems, consult your physician.

I met a guy down in Georgia who ran 10 miles a day to prepare for his 2,100-mile hike. He felt so strong cardiovascularly that he charged up and down those steep Georgia mountains. He badly injured his knee on one descent and had to abandon his journey after only a few days. A plastic kneecap was inserted and he was told that he could never backpack again.

If you have some extra weight on you, it will feel like twice as much when you're carrying a heavy pack. I always seem to be a good five pounds overweight. When I shoulder that pack for the first time in awhile, and make a mental note of all that is in there that maybe I could get rid of and come up with nothing except that extra weight on my body, I truly resent it. As much as I'd like to, I never seem to be able to shed it before I go. If you have more willpower than I do, it's not a bad idea.

Some thin people like to put *on* weight if they are planning a long trip. Todd always did. He could never carry enough food to satisfy his enormous appetite. He hiked over 20 miles every day (that was before he was married and got me for a partner), which required even more fuel than the average 12- to 15-mile day that most people hike.

Begin to pack for an extended backpacking trip well in advance so you don't forget anything. Keep a checklist handy or keep most of your gear, large and small, in one area or box so you can quickly grab it for a spontaneous overnighter. Repair any broken equipment. Sharpen your pocket knife. Replace moleskin and bandaids in your first aid kit. Water-seal your boots. Cut your toenails. Check your tent's seams for peeling seam seal. Check to see if you ever cleaned your pots and pans. On an overnighter, we never bother to clean our pans until we get home. It is so much easier in a sink with hot running water and dish soap.

One time, however, when I was single, my lawyer friend asked to borrow my cook-kit and stove for a canoe trip he was planning. I had been trying to get him interested in me for a long time but never had any luck. When I brought the cook-kit and stove up to his office to show him how to operate it, it was full of green mold when I took it out of its sack. I had packed it away and forgot to clean it. Well, I left an impression on him, but not the kind I had hoped for! You don't need those sort of surprises on your hike, either.

These chores should be done *after* you come home from a trip and before you pack your gear away. But check it all out before you leave again, just in case you forgot.

If you are making a new dish on the trail, try it out at home first.

Now for the hike itself. Once you decide on the area you want to hike in, acquire the necessary maps and guidebook. It's not a bad idea to give the officials (park superintendent, forest service ranger, or trail club overseer, et cetera) a call and check on the condition of the trail you're interested in hiking. Bridges may have been washed out because of high water. Sections may be closed because of forest fire. A hurricane may have gone through and knocked down many trees across the trail. A steep trail section may have gotten washed away. Lingering snow could make the high country impassable. You don't need to live far away from the trail you are planning to hike on to be unaware of major changes like these. An upstate Pennsylvania trail was closed one year because of a hurricane—a very localized one—and we never knew until we got there.

There are other things to inquire about, too. High-water fords that would make you want a pair of sneakers along for crossing. A drought may have caused the "reliable" water sources to dry up and make you want to carry an extra water bottle. High fire danger may prohibit you from having a campfire and so you must be sure to carry your backpacking stove. Or perhaps no one has gotten a chance to maintain the trail lately, and it is overgrown or difficult to follow, or merely not fun to hike on. In all cases, you could change your mind about where to hike before you left home.

Planning Your Itinerary

Begin planning when you leave the house. The time it takes to travel to the trailhead must be included. If it takes you six hours of driving to arrive there, you will not be able to put in a full day's hike on that day, or the day in which you drive home. If you plan to drive through the night, you will probably suffer from road fatigue and lack of sleep the next day and will not want to put in a full day's hiking, either.

How many days or partial days are left? We like to plan about 8 to 12 miles the first full day, depending on the terrain and what kind of shape we are in. You can increase your mileage as the days go by, as you become stronger, and as your pack becomes lighter. On one occasion, three of our students went out on a 42-mile loop hike. The four days in which they had to do it was sufficient time to complete it. One member, however, thought it was best to start off with a 16-mile day. That way, "We get a good chunk of it under our belts and the rest should be a piece of cake." Well, that plan was far beyond the capabilities of another member of the group. Because she felt it necessary to go along with the plan and did not speak up when planning the itinerary, she fell apart, physically and emotionally, and this resulted in the entire hiking party having to abandon the trip.

When planning your daily mileage and possible camp spots, study the map's topo lines and data to determine the best places. Will you have an all-day climb from your valley starting point to get to the ridge? Plan a short first day then. Will one stretch be a long, flat ridgewalk? That day, you could probably do a lot of miles. Don't schedule a long, steep climb in the heat of the day. Plan to camp at the bottom, if possible, and climb first thing in the cool of the morning. Is there a gradual, long descent on the last day? You ought to be feeling good enough to finish off with a big day. How about a stretch with lots of vistas or a lake with possible swimming? Although you may be *able* to do a lot of miles that day, it may be more enjoyable to do some rock-sunbathing instead.

There are other things to consider when planning your mileage, such as the weather forecast. Is it calling for inclement weather? A steady, cold rain can make your normal mileage impossible to cover. You may need to hole up in your tent until a thunder and lightning storm passes or quit hiking early in the day because of one. Build some down-time into your schedule.

When planning your mileage and destination points, if possible, have two options in mind for a short day and a long day. The more flexibility you build into your schedule, the more assured you can be of reaching your goal.

After your on-the-trail days are planned, allow for enough time at the end to get out to the trailhead and drive home. Examine the maps and guidebook for alternate routes, side trails, and logging and fire roads that would enable you to shorten your hike should you run into trouble. Locate roads that cross the trail which might allow you to hitchhike back to the car should you need to get out. The map will tell you what grade the road is, which will help you determine if there will be much traffic traveling it. Without this information, you could sit a long time on a gravel road, or even a small blacktop back road, waiting for a ride.

Resupplying on the Long Trail

Any backpacking trip longer than a week will be more enjoyable if a resupply stop is planned. There are two ways to do this. One way is to pick up your supplies when you go into a town nearby the trail, buying everything en route. You can often expect to pay saltier prices at these small rural general stores, and your options and variety may be severely limited. This may force you to make a long hitch to a larger town in search of an obscure item.

The other method is to mail a box of supplies addressed to yourself, General Delivery, to the post office in a town near the trail. Your pack will remain lighter, because your supply quantities will be smaller.

Depending on the length of your trip, many resupply boxes may need to be packed before departure. Your "ground control" support person back at home, who will coordinate mailing the resupply boxes and final packing, is of the utmost importance. Choose someone who is super-reliable, who is interested in your trip, and who lives relatively close to a post office. Some boxes of supplies may need to be shipped immediately, so cooperation is essential. Your boxes should be lined up in the order they should be mailed, left open, and a note should be attached to each stating the post office's address, your expected arrival date, what to add to that box's contents at the last minute, and the date that it should be mailed. In addition to your resupply boxes, a large box of extra general supplies should be available to your support person. When your trail supplies need to be replaced, you can call home and request these items be placed in your next outgoing box.

A large part of your resupply box will contain food. If possible, a combination of store-bought fresh food like good bread, cheese, a green pepper or an apple, along with dry trail-type food is best for variety and nutritional balance. Buy ahead of time the trail food that is difficult to find (such as freeze-dried), or is available only in larger quantities (such as instant dried milk), or at a savings, and pack it in the quantities needed for each individual supply drop.

If possible, plan your food drops between five and ten days apart, depending on the close proximity of towns and the ease of getting there. Less than five days, you'll spend too much time off the trail and will run into more weekends and closed post offices. Over ten days, your pack will become unbelievably heavy.

When deciding on quantities of food for each drop, figure the number of days you'll need to cover those trail miles between towns. Examine the terrain, expected trail conditions, and forecasted weather when deciding the number of miles you plan to cover. Build in safeguards for inclement weather, unexpected diffi-

culties, soreness, et cetera, that could make one trail section longer to cover than another. Remember that you may eat breakfast early and dinner late, leaving about 12 hours for lunch and snack foods. And in colder weather you will burn more calories, necessitating more food.

When you decide on your pace, add enough food for one full extra day to each resupply box for emergencies. You can use it on a layover day in a downpour, or eat extra food at the end of the stretch, or give it to another hiker if you don't need it. It's a good idea to add at least one freeze-dried supper to each box for late nights, extreme fatigue, or water shortage. Double-bag any powders to prevent puncturing and spilling and pack any liquids in an additional plastic zip-lock bag.

One of the best ways of packing and mailing liquids or small items is to go to your local photography store and ask for empty 35mm film containers. They are usually abundant and free, and some brands' containers are transparent, revealing the contents' level. It is not recommended that you use these containers for food, however, because they have chemical residue in them that cannot be washed out. You can either carry those film containers or add their contents to a better or larger bottle that you always carry in your pack. For supplies like biodegradable soap, carry a container with a squirt nozzle, which can be picked up at a drug-store. These small bottles are sold with hand lotion, shampoo, et cetera, for travelers, and can be used up, washed out, and refilled. Saline solution and disinfectant for contact lenses can be carried in smaller labeled and sterilized contact cleaner bottles. The cleaner can be put into an even smaller sample bottle available upon request from your eye doctor.

Some items to consider putting in your resupply boxes:

- vitamins—precounted for each stretch
- toilet paper—half rolls that were taken off the holder and collected in advance, saving pack space
- boot grease/leather conditioner
- toothpaste
- salt and pepper and spices
- contact solutions
- oil/soy sauce

- lotion for dry conditions
- liquid biodegradable soap and shampoo
- map and guidebooks of upcoming territory
- film and developing mailers
- laundry detergent—premeasured and triple-packed in plastic bags away from food
- flashlight/headlamp batteries and bulbs
- candles
- hair elastics, bobby bins, barrettes
- matches/lighter
- extra zip-lock plastic bags
- writing paper, envelopes, stamps, pen

In addition to frequently used items, occasional supplies may be needed on longer trips. Place them in your box at regular intervals (every month), or have them available in your general supply box for adding upon your request. Some occasional supplies to consider:

- first aid resupply
- reading book
- bug dope
- new journal
- extra camera lens, filters, lens paper
- new underwear, socks, T-shirt
- change-in-season clothes and equipment
- tape for packing boxes to mail home equipment no longer needed
- padded envelopes for mailing back used guidebooks/maps, and for your "ground control" person to mail you small things
- bootlaces
- tampons/panty liners/sanitary napkins
- traveler's checks
- suntan lotion

Last-minute items to add before a box is closed include film (stored in the freezer to discourage deterioration), and any food like homemade jerky which will stay fresher if left frozen until the last minute. Laundry detergent should not be packed until the very end, either. If for some reason your trip is interrupted or postponed for any great length of time, take out any items with fragrance so the odor is not absorbed by the food.

Lists of towns and post offices are available from some trail organizations, helping you decide which ones to mail packages to. Or study the map and guidebook for road crossings and nearby towns with post offices and stores. Send a note to each postmaster with a self-addressed, stamped post card requesting days and times that office is open for business. Inquire about the shipping schedule from your local post office for the number of days a parcel-post package will take to travel between postal zones. Take weekends and holidays into consideration when planning your schedule and allow extra time for your box to get to small towns. Be very generous with the lead time on your box. You don't want to sit and wait for it to arrive, often without food and money. Address your box:

Your Name
General Delivery
Harper's Ferry, WV *(or appropriate address for other post
    offices)*
Please hold for AT HIKER *(or PCT HIKER, or whatever trail is
    planned)*
Expected arrival date—8/9/92

You often need a photo ID to pick up your box, so carry a photo license. Post offices will generally hold a box (and mail) for three weeks before mailing it back to the return address.

PART

II

OUT THERE

▲ ▲ ▲ ▲ ▲ ▲ ▲ ▲ ▲ ▲

CHAPTER

Hiking the Trail

▲ ▲ ▲ ▲ ▲ ▲ ▲ ▲ ▲

*I*f you stand on the Appalachian Trail in any one spot, and look either north toward Maine or south toward Georgia, you should see one white paint blaze, and maybe even several, on the trees before you. Follow them, and they will take you to the trail's farthest end ... little white painted guideposts. When you're hiking and you don't see one in awhile, you could get panicky and wonder if you've lost the trail. "Have you seen any blazes lately?" you may ask your comrades, with whom you were probably involved in a deep conversation and forgot to continue watching. You'll continue in the same direction for awhile, actively looking ahead now for a sign that you're going in the right direction and turning around to see if there are any going the other way.

When a trail is blazed, you become very dependent on the blazes for direction. We realized this while hiking the Pacific Crest Trail after we already did the Appalachian Trail, where there are often no trees to paint blazes on if the trail builders wanted to. On the Appalachian Trail, you had to depend on your data, your compass, and your good sense.

I hiked with a greenhorn down in Georgia who was so uptight about staying on the trail that he walked with the opened guidebook in his hand. Every tenth of a mile's worth of data he absorbed and noticed. It's hard to believe he had any time or energy to notice anything else, like beauty, along the way.

My AT partner never picked her head up when she first began hiking, which is a common practice of the inexperienced: foot watching. I would hide in the bushes at trail intersections (an-

90

nounced by painted *double* blazes), and call to her after she missed the turn. "Look for the blazes," I'd tell her. I didn't want her to get lost and the opportunity was there many times a day.

Following a blazed trail is somewhat like driving a car. There are lots of things coming into your plane of vision. On the highway, it's the cars. On the trail, it's the beauty of the natural world, and your ever-present inner thoughts or conversation vying for your attention. As you hike, be mildly concerned with finding your way—as you'd glance at the speedometer or in your rear view mirror as you drive. Don't let finding your way consume you.

Focus your eyes ahead on the trail, not down by your feet. When you're looking ahead, the obstacles at your feet will still be in your line of vision, but you will also be able to take in that deer moving through the brush, that ray of sunlight spotting the trail ahead, *and* that double blaze announcing a turn. This may sound like the obvious, but over the years I have been amazed at how many people hike with their heads aimed downward.

We read our data periodically (at breaks) and are subconsciously aware of milestones to come—where the woods trail turns out to a woods road, where you hit the ridgeline and follow it, where you descend to a small pond. If it doesn't happen in the amount of time and miles passed that it should, we begin to actively look for it and check the data to see if we've made a mistake. These checks keep you aware of your surroundings and keep you heading correctly.

We've all at one time or another read our data and announced to our comrades something like this, "We have a 2-mile descent to reach the road." The point where you are is given as one elevation and the next point, 2 miles further, is lower. There is no data between those two points and so most will assume they will be descending the entire time. Occasionally, however, you may do some ascending in those 2 miles. Perhaps you will do a lot of ascending, or perhaps you will go over a series of knolls, until you make your final, hard descent. If it occurs at the end of the day, when you're feeling tired, you may not appreciate this "surprise."

Data does not always cover *every* elevation gain and loss. It is often summarized. To find out exactly what you will be doing, consult the topo map for a genuine look at what the trail will do. It can tell you if your trail contours for 1¾ of that 2 miles and then plummets down to your lower elevation. It will tell you if your descent is

very gradual the entire time. Locate yourself on the map and look at the topo lines that it crosses as the trail progresses. Find a number of elevation feet, which are printed periodically on some of the lines. Does the trail cross the lines quickly, meaning it is steep, or every inch or so, indicating a gradual descent? Does it cross in one direction, going down, and then change and go back up, before going back down again? That means there is a knoll stuck in the middle of that descent that you have to get over before your final descent. Studying the trail as it crosses over the topo lines will prevent such surprises.

On your hike, look at the topo map and the corresponding point on the trail often, perhaps every time you break. Look for road crossings and small black squares, indicating cabins or structures. Watch where the tree line stops on the map, indicating an open summit or ridge, or open meadow. Learn to see the land by looking at your map. Develop these skills when you know where you are, to assist you if you ever become disoriented. Get a good book on compass reading and practice using your compass the same way—when you're found. Carrying a compass does you little good if you don't know how to use it.

Natural Signs Showing Direction

Vegetation grows larger and more openly on northern slopes and smaller and more dense on southern slopes.

Moss thrives most thickly on the shadiest side of trees, which will be the north side if the trees are fairly in the open where sunlight can reach them all day.

The bark of poplar trees will be whiter on the south side and darker on the north side.

Snow will be more granular on the sunny south side of ridges, knolls, and mountains compared to the north side.

Evergreens tend to be bushier on the south side. This excessive growth is easiest to notice on trees that are growing apart from the others. Their tops also tend to point east.

Even if you have no compass, you can prevent yourself from traveling in circles when lost by always keeping two trees or objects lined up in front of you.

Game trails can be a tremendous aid to a lost person, if for nothing else than making traveling easier. They may lead to water in dry country and where they widen and deepen, the heavier traffic often means that the animals are going around a section of the terrain which is steep or boggy or somehow impassible. Always use game trails to travel on if they are heading in your desired direction and deviate from them when they go off your intended course.

You can tell direction by shadows if there is sunlight or moonlight strong enough to cast them. Drive a stake into the ground and mark the top of its shadow with a stone or a stick. Ten to fifteen minutes later, mark its shadow again. A line drawn from the second shadow to the first will point generally west in the northern hemisphere.

Stars can be used to tell direction because of the earth's rotation as the heavens rotate from east to west in great arcs. Drive two pegs into the ground with their tops lined up with a bright star, and observe over a period of a few minutes. If the star appears to

be falling, it is positioned west of you. If it appears to be moving to the right, you are facing south. Rising, and you are facing east. Moving to the left, and you are facing north. Take several readings and mark which direction is north so you can head in the correct direction come morning.

Pace

Everyone has his or her own pace. Mine is steady and slow. I take my time and usually don't burn out. I hike long days and still cover a substantial number of miles. I discovered my true pace—2 to 2½ miles an hour—when I realized that I hiked at the same speed whether I had a loaded pack on or was only day hiking. It is the speed I need to go in order to satisfy my desire to look around *and* cover ground. I am certainly capable of going faster and will if I need to, but then I will sacrifice the experience that I treasure. If I try to absorb where I am traveling and go at a faster pace, I end up tripping and do not enjoy myself as much.

Before Todd and I got together, his pace was much faster. He would get his 10 miles in way before lunch when hiking the AT, and finish up his 20-plus-mile day by 3:00 P.M. Then he'd sit in the shelter the rest of the day. Twenty miles was far enough to go, he figured. He was a youngster when he hiked the AT—eighteen or nineteen years old. Younger hikers tend to hike at a faster pace. They often get caught up in the physical aspect of the hike and want to see how their body performs and discover its limits. This motivates older hikers, too—they're just not driven to the same degree.

When Todd met me, all that changed. Besides the fact that he wanted to be with me whether we talked as we hiked or just stayed close enough to share an experience—an eagle soaring overhead, or a coyote slinking across the trail—he couldn't get me to hike much faster. I did if I had to and it never ceased to amaze him what kind of pace I could crank out. It wasn't my choice to hike fast, though. It didn't make me happy, it defeated my purpose for being there, and so he slowed down.

When most people form a partnership on the trail and share community weight, their pack weight usually decreases. Todd's increased, on purpose, for a few reasons. He took more of the community weight. The weight slowed his pace down to become closer to mine. Not every partner will agree to do this. There usually needs to be some deep love involved before you can get a partner to consent, but it can work. The more weight carried, the slower the pace. Carrying more weight made him hungrier. Going slower made us cover fewer miles and, hence, made us need more food to get to the resupply point. *And* his wife was a much better trail cook than he, so it was worth carrying more and better food, such as a whole bag of spices and herbs.

We ran into trouble on some ascents—the place I really slow down and where he likes to kick out a steady, hard pace to reach the top. He normally hikes behind me, to hold himself back, or he would take off uncontrollably and perhaps get too far ahead. On ascents, however, the spacing between us seems to shrink and I feel like I am a cow being prodded. I often encourage him to pass and meet me at the top. We are both often happier when we split up. The frustration cools in us both by the summit. And there are times when you simply want to be alone. When we hiked in the Sierra Nevada in 1988, my mother had just died before we departed.

I had not fully realized her death and I needed to talk to her while I hiked. Even though Todd was respectfully quiet behind me, I wanted to be alone a lot. I encouraged him to pass and would say, "You can go ahead, honey," but he often didn't want to. I had to come right out and ask him and tell him I needed to be by myself, which was hard for me to do. Even an extroverted hiker like myself needs solitude at times, let alone the typical introverted hiker.

Finding Your Pace

An important tool to assist you in finding your pace is a watch. We don't like to be reminded of the time normally, so we keep it concealed in a fanny pack, only pulling it out to get an idea of the passing day. Wearing it can be too much of an intrusion. I hiked in Georgia with a man who received a watch as a going-away present from the bank where he worked. It had a beeper which he set for noon. When it went off, we had to sit down and have lunch, no matter where we were, smack on the trail itself, even if a beautiful view was half a mile farther down the trail. That practice didn't last long.

It's wise if a hiker knows how to judge time passing on the trail by a sense of the number of miles he or she covers and the speed at which he or she is moving. When my partner, Colleen, and I started the AT, we did not have a watch. We had to cover about 7 or 8 miles to get to the first shelter. It was drizzling. No sun was visible to tell us how many hours of sunlight remained. Every time we descended into a deep gap, it appeared to be getting dark. We got frantic that the day was drawing to a close and we still weren't at the shelter and began to hurry. When we got on top of the next summit, it was much brighter and we relaxed a bit. The next dark gap made us step on it again. We hiked those 7 miles feeling frantic much of the time, for we really had no clue how much daylight remained. A watch would have enabled us to enjoy our day so much more.

If it's important that you reach your planned destination by nightfall, a watch can help you keep a handle on the passing day so you can set your pace accordingly.

Interruptions affect your ability to judge the amount of time and miles passed. The more frequently you stop, whether it's to sit for a break, to look at flowers or birds, or just to pause for a breather on a hard climb, affects the amount of ground you cover. It's very difficult to sense how much ground was covered, even if you have a watch.

The best way to learn your pace is to choose a point down the trail—say, a spring that's 2 miles away. If you arrive in 1 hour, you were hiking at a 2-mile-per-hour pace. If you need to look for a water source in ¾ mile, you know you should arrive there in about 20 minutes at that pace. If after 25 minutes you still don't reach it, you can begin to question if you passed it. You can then go back, if you desire, to locate it before you get too far away. Once you develop a good sense of the passing time and the mileage together, you will need to consult your watch less frequently.

If you know the feel and speed of your normal pace, say 2 miles per hour, you will also learn to judge what pace is 3 miles per hour, and what pace is 1 mile per hour. When there are 8 miles remaining and only 3 hours of daylight, you will have to shift your pace closer to 3 miles per hour. On very hard climbs, you will be able to say, "We're traveling 1 mile per hour; we'll have to make it up onto the flat ridge or down the descent in order to get to our camp tonight." Knowing your pace is a safety factor—and a watch is a very important tool to help you develop it.

Hiking with a Partner

I am an extroverted person—extremely extroverted. There aren't many serious long-distance hikers who are. According to Dr. O.W. Lacy, who conducted a Myers-Briggs personality test on AT thru-hikers, most people who seek that type of experience enjoy and need their time alone.

Before I got my "permanent partner," my husband, Todd, I used to attract and encourage hikers to join in my company. They felt like an extended family to me, for you can get very close to the people that you share so many experiences with. Who wants to go out dancing when you hit a resupply town if you are hiking alone? All-you-can-eat restaurants are more enjoyable with a few starved comrades in your company. Hiking by a lake can turn into a beach party if there are friends with you. And would you really impersonate Gene Kelly by belting out "Singin' in the Rain" and dancing down the wet trail if you were doing a solo? You'd probably become quiet, glum, and maybe even self-pitying if there was no one to help lift your spirits.

Hiking with a partner is definitely not for everyone. Sometimes, hikers choose to join forces for other reasons than socializing. When Todd arrived at the Mexican border on the Pacific Crest Trail, he was alone. As he neared the snowbound Sierra Nevada, however, he and a few other hikers began to stick together. They felt it would be easier and safer to have more than one set of eyes search for a route and assist in river fords, traverses, et cetera. Rather than doubling up in tents, cooking together, and sharing community gear, they opted for a looser commitment in order to keep their independence and freedom. They all carried a full load as if they were hiking solo. This sense of independence kept them together as a group and also gave them time alone when they desired it.

Personally, I like more of a commitment from a partner. Before I was married, I planned to stay with my female partners throughout the duration of the hike. Only one tent, stove, et cetera, was taken between us. It didn't always work out. One of my partners did indeed leave. Another wanted to for a while but decided against it. All the other partnerships were very successful. A good trail partnership takes more than hard work. It takes a certain amount of chemistry.

Differences in hiking pace is not the number one reason that most partners split up, but rather clashes in personality. Look closely at your personality traits and characteristics and try to assess if you tend toward being extroverted or introverted. If you really enjoy and need your private space and time, keep this in mind when choosing your partner. Someone who likes to chat, or stick close to other people, or who is uncomfortable being alone, may conflict with your needs.

Resentment can build up and conflicts can erupt if each individual is not given separate space or time alone on occasion. It is important to tune in to your partner's nonverbal communication if he or she does not come right out and ask for this space. Clues can often be picked up by a sudden quietness or sense of distance from your partner. Always make the opportunity for talk in case your partner needs to vent. If your partner doesn't take your bite, he or she may just need to be left alone. Often, that is all that is

needed to keep a partnership together—shared respect for each other's private thoughts and space.

If your and your partner's paces are different, there are ways to adjust and adapt your pace and style so you can stay together. Not too many partners are fortunate enough to have the exact same pace. And even if they do, it can vary from day to day, depending on how an individual is feeling, physically and psychologically. My Appalachian Trail partner, Jo Ann, and I did not have the same pace. She always shot ahead in the mornings. I plodded slow and steady. Since she was new at hiking, every aspect of it fascinated her. She would stop right on the trail and record her feelings, whether it was about her aches and pains or the new flower in front of her. Meanwhile, her slower partner would catch up. Sometimes she got into camp early and read. Other times, she just soaked in the view and spent time thinking about where she was and how she was changing. Some minor problems can arise from this well-working arrangement. If too long a time has elapsed, the waiting partner may be really ready to get up and get going, just as the slower partner is coming over the horizon. In our case, however, since my pace was more relaxed, I didn't feel like I needed a lengthy rest when I did catch up. You do need to each compromise and meet halfway. A partnership will not work if you don't. It is good practice for life—and gives you some ideas for working a marriage.

There are some hikers who find that the peace and solace of the natural world is exactly what the doctor ordered for their personalities and their lifestyles, and they frankly cannot or will not bend and work together in a partnership. Once they have become expert hikers, these solitary types are much better off taking to the hills solo.

When you are in a partnership sharing communal gear, extreme effort must be made so that you arrive at the same camp spot at the end of the day. It could be disastrous for one or even both members if you became separated. Plan an alternate campsite a few miles shy of your first-choice camp site. Meet there and discuss if you both want to or are able to continue farther. Your partner may be having difficulty just reaching the first site. Actually, it is a good idea to check in with each other a few times throughout the day.

No matter how you split up communal gear, each individual should always carry his or her own water, snacks that do not require cooking, rain gear, sleeping bag, et cetera. It only makes sense for the person who is carrying the stove to be also carrying the supper bag. (However, the person who is *not* carrying the tent should carry the ground cloth and the cord/rope. If they do become separated, that person would then have adequate shelter for the night.)

Todd and I ran into some trouble like this when we were hiking with some of our friends on the Pacific Crest Trail. We often sat around on breaks talking and laughing to such an extent that we'd have to race at the end of the day to reach our destination. Since I was considerably slower than everyone else, I would end my break early and hike ahead. Once, they lost track of time and did not catch up to me for hours. In that time, I went from being concerned to frantic, to very angry, when I finally saw them coming. Todd had the guidebook and the map. He also had the lunch and the water; he told me he'd take care of it so my pack would be lighter. I was extremely thirsty, hungry, and worried that I was not on the right trail. (There were no signs telling me which way to go at intersections.) I felt incredibly foolish, too, for being so dependent.

Partners do not always have duplicates of maps and guidebooks, but share one between them. If your commitment to each other is rather loose, it would be a good idea to have your own set. Partners need to stick even closer together if they are sharing one set. Some hikers leave messages to those behind communicating which way they have gone. Arrows made out of sticks or rocks can be constructed at intersections. Notes on scraps of paper can be left under a rock. In this case, the faster hiker should have the guidebook or map—or he or she will have to wait for his slower partner, which actually is a better idea. I was once in a group that foolishly had to follow two other members down the wrong trail for many, many miles. We had a boy with us whose father was ahead and they needed to be together come nightfall. They left arrows, all right, and we angrily kicked each one apart as we continued knowingly down the wrong path. They were misreading the data but not only were they certain they were correct, they did not feel the need for our input or calculations. This infuriated us, for we felt like a bunch of mindless sheep who could only follow.

It is always best to wait for your partner at any intersection where there is any degree of uncertainty. Your partner may miss even the most obvious intersection and run the risk of separation. Decide between yourselves how you will handle those situations. But if you choose to have the faster hiker make those decisions solo, expect to deal with anger and resentment from the partner who is following. Everyone likes to be included and feel like an equal.

There are many other things of which you will only need one between you and your partner: stove, cook kit, fuel, tent, ground cloth, first aid kit, repair kit, water bag, water filter, and rope. Each of your loads can be diminished by five pounds if you take advantage of sharing and splitting communal gear.

Sharing communal gear usually means that the community chores should also be shared. The chores that can be divided are setting up the tent, cooking, washing dishes, fetching water, purifying water, hanging food, taking down the tent, and retrieving food. Todd and I each have our own separate chores to do, just as we do in our normal life. We each tend to do the jobs we are best at or enjoy the most. I like to cook supper, so while I am doing that he gets water and prepares for the night by setting up the tent and laying out our bags. When you get into camp at the end of the day, unless there is a great deal of time to play with, the most pressing chores need to be done first. Therefore, we usually deal first with starving stomachs, thirsts, and the tent, if darkness is falling. Sometimes we switch when we grow fatigued of our chore or are not in the mood. It is always nice to give each other a break on occasion and if the person who usually fetches water has had an extremely hard time that day, be kind enough to offer to do it for him or her. This kind of consideration will take your hiking partnership much farther down the trail.

There are some chores which are simply not enjoyed by anyone, such as covering your packs in the middle of the night if it begins to rain and you've neglected to protect them, or chasing off marauding animals. Make sure you take turns and put as much energy into keeping it as fair as you can.

Mealtime could be another touchy subject when it comes to dividing the food you eat. My husband is bigger than I am, carries more weight, and burns more calories. By rights, he should get more food than I do, and he does. But when it comes to dividing our pasta with clam sauce, I want the option of getting my half, my fair share. If I can't eat it, which I often can't, he gets some of it transferred to his bowl. But if I am hungry enough, I eat it all and he has to look for something else to eat, like a cheese sandwich or a handful of cereal. That way, I don't miss out on the best food. This has always worked for us—right down the middle. The one who doesn't divide the food gets to choose first, just like with children.

How to Find a Partner

One place to find a partner is your local hiking club. Join them for a few of their scheduled hikes and meet some prospective partners. Or try to get a friend interested in the sport—someone with whom you already have a good rapport. You're one step ahead by choosing someone you already know.

Some organizations publish newsletters or magazines that carry advertisements for hiking partners. It will include a subscription to their magazine/newsletter in which you can advertise for a partner, or write to those already listed.

Appalachian Trail Conference
Appalachian Trailway News Magazine
P.O. Box 807
Harper's Ferry, WV 25425
(304) 535-1331

Appalachian Long Distance Hikers Association
Coordinator
197 Big Spring Rd. SE
Calhoun, GA 30701

Pacific Crest Trail Conference
The Communicator
365 W. 29th Ave.
Eugene, OR 97405
(503) 686-1365

I had an unfortunate experience hooking up with a man via the mail. He was thirty years older, which didn't bother me. We had corresponded for six months prior to my Pacific Crest Trail trip. In his letters he sounded competent. My male friends who read his letters, however, were very concerned that he had an ulterior motive beside wanting to share trail miles. I grew concerned when we began talking on the phone because he referred to me as "Babe." He seemed awfully chummy and suggestive for a stranger. But I wanted company badly.

When we met at a coffee shop in San Diego, I knew my intuition and friends had been right. He had close-cropped white hair, double-knit "hiking pants," a polo shirt pulled taut over his potbelly, and new boots with "only 40 miles on the tread," he said. "I want to save the soles." As we talked at the coffee counter, he stuck his face close to mine. His eyes bulged out of his head. His teeth were rotten. I felt nauseated.

We parted ways before we even got on the trail. He was crazy when I told him my decision. "Let's try it for a week!" he begged. "Oh, I know it can work. Just give me a chance. Trust me."

My girlfriends and I pulled his ninety-pound pack out of the car trunk, complete with rope, hatchet, shovel, and saw, and I said, "I'm sorry."

He got off the trail only two days later. He told another hiker it wasn't what he expected.

If your prospective partner was discovered through the mail, put a great deal of energy into getting to know him or her before an extended hike. An overnighter or even a day hike will tell you a tremendous amount about that person. Your personalities may clash violently. You may get enough of an idea that there is a great possibility that things may not work out between the two of you. You can prepare ahead of time to hike solo. *Always* have a back-up plan when you have a partner in case it does not work out. Some-times, even a married partner may have to decide whether to con-tinue alone if his spouse decides to abandon the trip en route.

Group Hiking

I went on my first organized hike with a hiking club when I was fif-teen years old. About a dozen people were along and we went about 15 miles. I can remember rushing the entire time—just trot-ting along the trail. My two friends and I weren't very prepared, equipment-wise, even though you don't need much for a day hike. What we did have—our water container—was poor. It was a gallon picnic thermos with carry strap that broke in the first few miles and it had to be carried in our arms the rest of the day. I really en-joyed hiking but not at that pace and not with such a large group. I joined the club for years, though, because I was too young to drive and they always met at a preliminary spot and carpooled to the trailhead. I learned a lot about the sport through the members' ex-

periences and I made some silly mistakes in their secure presence. As soon as I was old enough, I went my own way.

I couldn't seem to get away from hiking in groups, though. I draw hikers to me naturally as a result of my extroverted nature. I do prefer to bring them together myself, though.

For most people, group hiking is definitely the hardest way to travel. The more people in the group, the more varied the personalities, the more opinions, the more discussions, the more compromises, the more problems and conflicts, the more injuries, the more equipment breakdowns, et cetera. It's too much to deal with for most, but many people are in a situation where they must travel in a group, such as boy and girl scouts, church groups, 4-H, hiking clubs, et cetera.

Much of Todd's and my group experience has resulted from our 4-H job. We've also hiked in groups of adults as backpacking teachers at our local college, but our twelve-year-olds have taught us the most. With them, the dynamics were obvious and extreme. Most times, they were more open and up-front about the cause of the conflict, and were quick to forget it and move ahead. And when it comes down to it, many adults don't behave much differently.

Life in a group can be made much easier and even enjoyable by following a few practices. Aim to keep your group small (six to eight). If this isn't possible, you can diminish its size and impact by breaking up into two groups. One group can begin at one end of the trail, and the other at the opposite end. Care must be taken in choosing the camping spot if it is shared by both groups, to reduce impact. You can exchange car keys at a halfway meeting point to eliminate shuttling.

One person is always needed to coordinate the group—usually the most experienced or most knowledgeable about the area. Try to include as many others in the group in the planning stage, however. Everyone appreciates their opinions being valued, and it will help the members feel more included and equal. Someone may need to present the options once on the trail—choices to camp, miles to cover—and then allow the group to decide as a whole. This can be done at intervals as needed as the trip unfolds.

It is important to check with each person to make sure he or she has the necessary gear prior to departure—rain gear, for example, even if the weatherman is calling for clear skies. This is especially important with the inexperienced members who may easily forget to pack an important item. It can happen to old-timers, too, if lines of communication get crossed: "*I* was to bring the tent? I thought we always used yours." Remember that one member's shortsightedness may directly affect everyone else—three people stuck in a two-person tent, or having to bail out early because sudden rains are soaking the hiker with no rain gear.

Sometimes just carrying the gear isn't enough—it has to be used. We had a rain-gear problem with some young girls in our 4-H backpacking class. We made sure they had rain gear along, but we didn't know that it looked stupid to them, too stupid to wear. They carried it and they put it on when it rained, but as soon as they got behind us on the trail, they pulled out their more fashionable over-sized cotton sweatshirts and used them for warmth and "protection" from the rain. In a matter of minutes, they were soaked and freezing cold and had to abandon their week-long adventure.

If you know someone is not very experienced, it is a good idea to go through his or her equipment to see if he or she has everything that's needed and is not bringing anything that's unnecessary. Our 4-H twelve-year-olds don't always like this. The boys may be embarrassed for us to see their eight pairs of underwear when they're only going to be out for four days, or their cigarettes, and the girls, their mousse, make-up, hair spray, and deodorant. We always catch a few kids trying to smuggle portable cassette players along. It's a camp rule that no cassette players or radios are allowed. Radios violate your comrades' sense of space and take away their choice for peace and quiet.

When *Backpacker* magazine hired me to coordinate its first staff backpacking trip, I went through the packs and gear of the folks who weren't very experienced or totally inexperienced. It takes some humility to allow someone to do that, because for every questionable piece of gear or item, I had to ask what it was for and if it was necessary and then decide if it was important enough to be included. That's what an experienced backpacker does at every town stop, when he or she leaves town and shoulders that suddenly amazingly heavy pack.

On every climb on a long hike, week after week, resupply after resupply, I mentally went through every piece of gear to try to find something to get rid of to lighten my load. Down in Georgia, on the AT, you can hike the first 50 to 100 miles and find perfectly good gear abandoned on the trail and in the shelters because its added weight did not justify keeping it. The staff of *Backpacker* magazine were very happy for my intrusion once they got on the trail and had to actually carry their loads.

You would be wise to make a quick check of everyone's physical state as you prepare to leave. Is anyone recovering from an illness? Is anyone grossly out of shape, or are there any past histories of knee problems? These are things to prepare for in the event that they could experience a flare-up. Perhaps you will be traveling in a mountainous area with a lot of steep ascents and descents. That hiker with the weakened knee should carry a set of knee braces. My AT partner recently had a bout with tonsillitis before embarking on our 1,000-mile hike. She neglected to take the prescribed amount of pills with her, and when her body reached a weakened condition on the trail, the germ quickly reattacked her throat. We had to get off the trail, go into a town, and locate a doctor to get more penicillin.

We had a woman in one of our backpacking classes who had a medical problem that she didn't reveal until the last minute. Our weekend trip was already planned. We arrived at the trailhead and began walking up the trail on a very slight incline. She said, "Oh, by the way, I have a respiratory disease. I'm not able to get winded." As we had to climb a mountain and carry full packs for two days, that would have been difficult to prevent. We took her pack back to the car, which was still in sight, and told her to day hike without her pack instead. Her announcement floored us. We wondered why she waited so long to tell us.

When planning your trip, always consider the possibility of *not* reaching your goal. Your chances of this happening increase proportionately as your group size increases. Many things can change en route: sudden illness or injury, extreme changes in weather (unseasonable snows, unceasing rains), or the challenge of the trail may simply be more than someone in the group can handle. Have alternative plans—a bail-out route such as a shorter loop that will take you back to your cars, a road crossing to hitch back on, or arrangements with a local or friend to pick you up prematurely.

Some of this can be avoided by not overestimating the number of miles you can cover. Figure the pace of the slowest member of your group and adjust your daily mileage accordingly. You may need to make some load adjustments if this is the only way your slower members can continue on. Shifting weight to a stronger or faster hiker is a possibility if all are in agreement.

Plan particular points along the course of your day, preferably at milestones such as creek fords, vistas, and summits where the party can regroup and check to see how everyone is doing. Things may have changed considerably for someone since the last meeting spot. The more check-in points you plan in your day, the greater your chances of avoiding potential problems. This way, each person is more free to go his or her own pace yet still enjoy the camaraderie of the group.

Someone who is experienced and very patient and helpful should bring up the rear in a group hike. His or her knowledge can keep minor problems from developing into dangerous situations.

As the day comes to a close, instruct the "eager beavers" out ahead on exactly where the campsite is located, or have the group stay together.

When hiking behind a person, always maintain a reasonable distance between the two of you so you do not walk into them if they suddenly stop to scratch their leg or study a flower. Walking too closely can also be dangerous since branches on an overgrown trail that are pushed aside by the person in front of you can spring back and swat you in the face. If you find the lack of space between you and the hiker behind you uncomfortable, ask him or her to either pass or give you a few more feet. When you're sharing conversation, however, you may want to close up that space between the two of you a bit. It is better to do this than to shout and bring noise pollution to the woods.

Our 4-H kids always have problems with this, as does nearly every group we've observed on the trail. They always get backed up and traffic becomes congested.

There are certain trail manners that you should observe. If someone comes upon you from behind, either step to the side of the trail or ask if they'd like to go ahead. To keep our 4-H kids off each others' heels, we make them stand in a line and have the second person count to twenty-five slowly before taking off after the first person. It creates enough space between them to give them the experience of being able to see ahead instead of seeing someone else's heels and backpack. After the first or second time they counted off, we caught them doing it on their own. We saw them make the guy behind stop (since he didn't want to pass), and count off, in order to create some breathing room.

A weekend on the trail will bring you in closer contact with your traveling companions than most married couples experience. A day of togetherness can last up to twelve or fourteen hours. Try very hard to be as sensitive, cooperative, and cheerful as possible. Strive toward harmony and avoid situations that cause friction. Put extra effort into getting along. A hiker can become cranky and irritable from soreness and fatigue. The kind of mood you exude will directly affect every other member of the group. Keep your complaining to a minimum and if you feel sour, keep it to yourself.

Never suffer silently, however. Many people in the rear have dragged themselves along, trying desperately to keep up and maybe even wiping away a tear or two as they try to cope. Speak up if you are really falling apart. It is difficult to express this sort of thing. It takes courage, and understanding companions. Often adjustments can be made to make it more bearable for you and insure that you and everyone else will be able to continue. If you don't speak up, you could injure yourself to the point where everyone may have to abandon the hike.

Before you decide to do something apart from the group—diving into a lake with an unknown bottom, setting off to scale a peak in inclement weather—think of how it will affect the rest of the group if you get into trouble. A group hike is no time for an individual to act selfishly. Don't take unnecessary risks or do anything foolish simply because there are others close by to bail you out.

Always chip in with group activities such as gathering firewood for a community campfire. Don't leave those chores for everyone else. People will notice if you are always occupied with your own personal chores or gear when the time arrives to lend a hand. They may not comment, but resentment could build up and disrupt the inner harmony of the group. Everyone appreciates a helpful person.

Hiking groups should not leave the responsibility of digging their own cat holes to each individual member. It is more sanitary to have someone dig a community hole. This way, each person does not have to be quizzed on sanitary methods. (Often they're not up to par.) Even if they are aware of the correct procedure, some do not practice it.

Groups have a tendency to "take over" certain areas on the

trail. I've stopped at a shelter or two in the rain where the spread-out group inside never consolidated themselves so we could take a break from the wet and cold. Or I've had to maneuver myself around and over bodies of groups of kids who took a break right on the trail itself and didn't so much as bend their legs or pull in their stuff sack of food so we could get by with greater ease. Keep your group somewhat separate from other trail users whenever you can. Avoid shelters, and tent off to yourselves. Many others come out seeking solitude and find groups disturbing. Keep your group's voices lower than normal, if possible. Their collected voices will multiply and sound louder.

Another place to be aware of your presence is public store-fronts, restaurants, and post offices. Try to think of ways to mini-mize your group's presence, not call attention to it.

One of the greatest advantages of group hiking is eliminating the need to ever leave your pack unattended. Pack theft occurs on the trails, especially in more populated areas. There is a campspot on the Appalachian Trail where hikers are continually ripped off. It is not by a road but back in the woods a few miles. It even hap-pens during the day when hikers go down to the spring to fill up their water bottles. A local must just know the area and take occa-sional walks in there looking for unfortunate souls. Never leave anyone's pack unguarded, not even to get water or hitch to town to resupply.

Solo Hiking

Most serious backpackers prefer to travel solo. It is the nature of the animal, since many long-distance backpackers are introverted people. Solo hiking is not recommended by any hiking organiza-tion, but it fulfills exactly what these folks go out there to find—personal solitude. They not only enjoy solitude, they need it to be happy. This type of person is quite accustomed to spending time with his or her own private thoughts and it takes a lot to get lonely.

I was forced to backpack solo once in my life, on the AT, when my partner and I split up. I had the chance to experience all those feelings that solo hikers experience by choice and thrive on—learning to be with yourself and the natural world, learning to depend on yourself, and perhaps your Creator. It was a wonderful experience. Thoughts ran out of my head and onto my journal pages like flowing water.

Although I've always felt at home in the outdoors and the natural world, I do not fully come alive until there are people there to share in it. I, personally, become lonely. My preference is a very intimate group—one to two others. Although, I must admit, a solo backpacking trip is beginning to look very attractive in this particular time in my life. With two small children, I don't often get a chance to hear what my head is saying. I've become a different person since motherhood has entered my life and I think it would be a good idea to know exactly who this person is again. There's nothing like being alone in the woods to help you learn.

A solo hike may be just the thing for doing some soul-searching and reflection. When you are at a crossroads in your life, or are going from one life passage to another, or have a particular problem that needs to be worked out, a solo hike can be an invaluable vehicle in helping you with it. Every year, there are dozens of thru-hikers on the AT who are in exactly that kind of state in their lives—in transition or seeking an answer. Most complete their hike with a much clearer understanding and some wisdom.

A journal can be a good friend with which to spend time by writing in the evening, if there are no other people with whom to converse. Solo hiking promotes private thoughts and a journal can be a tremendous help to organizing them and helping clarify what you are feeling.

It is a good idea to give some thought to the type of person you are and whether you truly enjoy spending your time alone or in the company of others. I discovered what kind of person I was by being placed in a solitary situation. I've always enjoyed my private time to create—to paint, write, sew, et cetera—when I am diving deeply into my inner self for self-expression. But when I am outdoors, I feel opened up. I feel passion and energy going out of myself and into the world and that is what I so desperately need to share with other human beings. Find out what your own personal needs are. Don't be surprised if they will vary.

I found that when I solo hiked, more people opened up their homes and hearts to me. They have invited me to dinner, offered a ride into town for supplies, or the chance to take a break and do my laundry. A few times, people have gone to work and left me alone in their home to finish repacking. "Just lock the door when you're ready to leave," they have told me. At first I was amazed. I am always deeply moved and touched by their generosity and trust. It is very important to be as gracious, respectful, and grateful a guest as you possibly can, to positively reinforce their belief that most hikers are good people and that most of mankind is, too.

Hiking solo is a time to learn about humility and the universal needs of all people. Do not be ashamed to ask for help if you need it. On the trail, you are without many of the things you are accustomed to. You may, on occasion, find yourself in a situation where you need something that you don't have: water from a spigot on a dry road walk; when you're sick or injured, medicine, or a ride to the doctor; food, because you figured wrong and you're desperately low in supplies and hungry; a ride to a shoe store because your boots just blew out. Be humble. Be honest. Reciprocate. Offer money for gas or in exchange for the groceries. In exchange for hospitality, offer to do a chore, like split some wood, sweep off the porch, entertain their child. That generous person will then be quick to offer to the next person. Jot them a short note of thanks after you've passed or once you've returned home.

If you are hiking solo, there are some basic safety precautions to take. It is especially important for a family member or close friend back home to have a copy of your itinerary. Your license number and a general description of the car you are taking to the trailhead could also be of use to the state highway patrol if they must locate you.

Be a little more concerned than usual with your personal safety when hiking solo. When you pass through a town and talk with people, don't broadcast where you are planning on spending the night. This is especially important when talking to passersby whom you haven't gotten a chance to know. If you see or meet others in the woods that you feel uncomfortable around, say in a shelter, do not plan to camp there, but continue hiking farther. Do not make it a habit to camp by a road or in an area that is heavily used and easily accessible and could be visited by late-night partiers.

You need to be a little more knowledgeable of medicine when you are venturing out on the trail alone. Take a Red Cross first aid course and know how to administer to yourself should you become ill or injured. Your first aid kit should be more substantial too, and have more of the items to care for yourself over a longer period of time, since there's a greater chance no one will be around to go for help.

Carry a whistle in your front fanny pack or around your neck in the event that you get injured and need to signal for help. Its sound will carry much farther than your voice and will last much longer, too.

Even though you are hiking solo, your actions and well-being affect your fellow hikers whom you meet along the way. If you disappear from the trail strangely or unexpectedly, they may feel it their duty to go look for you or at least inquire to your whereabouts. No person is alone out there if others know of his or her existence. Everyone has a moral responsibility to help others in need and to look out for each other.

Hiking Hints and Tips

If the days are very hot, it is sometimes nice to walk very early in the day and later into the evening when temperatures are coolest, thereby leaving the hottest part of the day open for a siesta. The same number of miles can be covered as in a normal day without a long break.

Your trip can be enhanced by being able to identify birds, trees, insects, flowers, et cetera, along the way. A small guidebook may be worth its weight to you if you enjoy this pastime. For birds and small animals, a small, lightweight pair of binoculars or a monocular can help you to see and identify them. Keep them handy by wearing them around your neck or carry in your front fanny pack for easy access.

Birdwatching is best early or late in the day, since birds are usually most active in the hours around dawn and sunset. Spring is usually the best season for seeing the greatest variety and for seeing the males in their colorful breeding plumage. Leaves are not yet on the trees at this time of year, making it easier to spot them. For easier identification, try to look for: distinguishing markings, bill shape, sound, shape and size, behavior, flight patterns, and habitat.

Try to take a short rest every hour or two, even if it's only for 5 to 10 minutes. It will rejuvenate you and keep you going farther in the long run.

Stretch your hamstrings, calves, and feet before hiking ... your shoulders and back muscles, too, can benefit from the slow movements and it can do much to prevent torn and tight muscles.

You can give your body a rest on extremely steep terrain while you are still hiking by pausing for a split second on every step. As your rear leg is extended behind you, let it bear your weight.

In high elevations, take advantage of good weather by hiking longer hours than normal. On level ground, take advantage of this surface to cruise long distances without a break.

Starting your day before or at sunrise gives you much more flexibility during the day. You'd be surprised how many miles you can do at the same pace by starting at sunrise and hiking to sunset.

There are three surfaces for walking: uphill—walking too fast causes muscle pulls and getting burnt out, heel blisters, and achilles tendonitis; downhill—walking too fast or too slow causes knee problems and shin splints, falls, sprained ankles, and toe blisters; level—walking long distances causes sore feet (especially on rocks).

Avoid overextending yourself. Extreme fatigue acts like a tranquilizing drug. Your thinking and judgment become impaired, and you can suffer injuries and falls. When you are tired, you tend to stumble more, and your reaction time is slower. To avoid extreme fatigue, don't plan too long a day. Plan to hike no more than an 8-hour day, and aim for hiking closer to 5 to 6 hours the first and second days of your trip.

Stay on the trail. People cut switchbacks beside trails to make the climb less long, but these shortcuts do nothing for the ecology. Stay on the trails and never cut any of your own.

Keep the trail narrow. Trails widen when hikers walk around muddy spots or other obstacles on the trail. The result is more mud and a wider trail. Stay on the trail to spare the earth. You can always clean your boots later if they become muddy.

Use your rain gear as a layer of warmth (jacket and pants work better than a poncho), especially when you're in camp and not exercising.

If you're hiking in shorts and your legs get chilly when you take a break, pull out your coated nylon pack cover and use it as a "throw" over your legs. It is very warm and is easy to pack and unpack.

To prevent cold air from bellowing into your bag when you roll over in the night, take your down vest, sweater, or pile coat and lay it across your neck and chest, tucking it in as a collar and acting as an air break.

The best way to keep your feet warm is to keep the rest of your body well covered. If your feet are cold, put on your hat.

Don't overdress when you're hiking. Sweating will wet your clothes and chill you. It is best to stop and take something off when you climb and add layers as you need them.

Remember that there are three ways to lose your body's heat: **radiation**—when heat merely leaves your body, especially those areas exposed to the elements; **conduction**—when you sit directly on snow or ice or handle cold objects like your gas bottle; and **convection**—when wind blows the heat away from the unprotected parts of your body. Keeping these in mind will help you be more aware of your actions and help you to stay warmer.

CHAPTER

In Camp

▲ ▲ ▲ ▲ ▲ ▲ ▲ ▲ ▲

*T*he light is slanting low in the forest. Your pack is starting to feel like it's been on your back for a few days straight, not just a few hours. You are more than ready for the day to be over—ready to take off your pack and leave it there, ready to release your feet from your boots, ready to cook up a feast of a supper. For the last half mile, your vision has been focused ahead—in the trees, looking for that brown roof on the shelter—the sign that the day is over. When you see it, your spirits lift and your pace quickens. Home—for the night.

Many of the places I've camped throughout my hiking life mean a lot to me. You can say, "Moxie Bald, Maine," and visions of sunrise in the fire tower drift back to me. Or say "Guitar Lake, California," and the cold, frozen, snowy world is as sharp as that morning years ago. The campsites under the highway underpasses and the sound of traffic, or the camps right on the trail with a cliff at our side because we got caught without a level spot—the weather, the people, even the menu drift back to me when I think of the campsites where I've slept over the years.

Your campsite does indeed feel homey once you spread out your gear, set up your bedroom, kitchen, et cetera. That is one of the largest joys of hiking and backpacking—being so free and mobile that you can lay your head down at a different spot on this beautiful earth every night. Every new camp finds you at home.

Choosing a Campsite

In these times of overcrowded trails and campsites, it is best to avoid popular areas, if possible, and go into the little-used areas. Avoid weekends and holidays when possible. There will be fewer people in the woods and on the trails, if you do. We saw a marked difference in the national parks after Labor Day was over and the children were back in school. Discover wildlife refuges to hike in and national monuments.

The older and more experienced we become, the less we want to be around other people when we go out backpacking. If we hiked the AT over again, as much as we like socializing, we would probably avoid sleeping in shelters as much as possible. Hikers snoring, dogs barking at critters through the night, the hikers that talk into the wee hours and the early risers that are cranking their stove-alarms at 5:00 A.M., leave you with little sleep. Weekends always seem to bring surprise guests into the woods, if you are camping in a popular area. Once Todd and I were camping 100 yards below a shelter on the AT. About 11:00 at night we heard this awful commotion in the woods ... loud voices and a metallic banging. Some teenage boys were rolling a keg of beer up the mountain for an all-night party. We slept little that night.

If you see signs of partying at a campsite—beer bottles, trash, et cetera—move to another area if time allows. The added miles may seem burdensome, but you get better rest in the long run.

Water isn't a requirement for a good campsite, although it certainly makes life easier. You consume a lot of water for cooking, washing dishes, washing yourself, rehydrating foods overnight, preparing breakfast, and collecting enough water to get you to the next source. Carrying it is an option if the campsite is a dry one or if you choose a scenic site, say on top of a mountain for a view of the sunset, where there happens to be no water. Reversing lunch and supper is an option here. You cook your dinner meal, which usually requires water for its preparation, during the day, when you get to a water source. Then you eat your dry lunch at the end of the day and you'll only need to carry enough water to wash it down.

When you get into camp, put your pack down and take a walk around to look for a campsite. Split up with your comrades and go

in different directions. You often want to settle for the first spot if your pack remains on, only to have to put your boots back on and gather your gear when someone finds a much prettier and flatter spot.

Choose well-drained or sandy campsites. Look your potential site over and try to determine whether, if there were heavy rains, your site would be in the course of a run-off. A spot that looks like it could soak up a lot of moisture is a good choice. Stay out of fragile meadows and remain 200 feet back from any water source, to prevent contamination of the water and to lessen your impact on the banks of the stream or the lake.

In insect season, camp on higher ground where you are exposed to a nice breeze that will keep pests at bay. For a sense of privacy, place your campsite a good distance away from other campers. In addition, you'll lessen your impact by not overcrowding an area.

At Your Campsite

If you have camp shoes along, take off your boots as soon as you decide on your camp spot or after you fetch water. Changing into them will not only feel wonderful after a day of hiking, it will help save the area from being trampled and prevent it from looking overused and scarred.

Locate your cooking area away from your sleeping area. Animals will be attracted to the small bits of food that you've spilled on the ground while you cooked and ate. If your cooking area is some distance from your shelter, you will be less disturbed in your tent.

When you decide on a tent spot, lay down your ground cloth and then lay your body on top of it before you put up your tent. You will then be sure which end is higher and where to put the head of your tent (uphill), if there is a slight slant. You will also be able to detect any lumps or bumps so you can move the tent to the right or the left to avoid a root, et cetera.

Never take your foot and sweep the ground of all its cover when you are clearing the ground of uncomfortable things. Instead, get on all fours and pick up the sticks, stones, and pine cones with your fingers and toss them to the side. Leave all pine needles and leaves in place. In the morning, the only telltale sign that somebody slept there will be the compacted leaves, which will fluff up by the end of the day.

Don't dig trenches around your tent when it rains, nor cut evergreen boughs for bedding. Do not change nor take anything away from the land at all.

Remove any fallen wood or low-hanging branches from your immediate tent site that could trip you or poke your eye once it gets dark. When you get up to relieve your bladder in the middle of the night, your flashlight beam will be pointing downward, not up in the air, where sharp branches are. This is more likely to occur in camps under thick evergreen trees.

Cover your pack with your pack cover or plastic garbage bag before you retire for the night, to protect it from rain, dew, and animals. Gather any items that you may need for the night and the next morning: flashlight, toilet paper, map and guidebook, hat, filled water bottle, pain relief, rain gear if it looks like rain, et cetera. Fluff up your sleeping bag before crawling inside. The air trapped within the fibers will warm you.

Before we get out of our sleeping bags in the morning, or at least break camp, we have a good idea where we will be sleeping next. We study the map and data, often in bed, and decide on the number of miles we'd like to cover and calculate where that will bring us. We often have two sites at two different mileage points picked out, in case we're feeling really strong and want to go farther. It's nice to have the option.

Campfires

Carry a stove for your cooking and keep campfires to a minimum. Observe fire warnings. No wind should be present when making a fire. *Low* fire conditions should be present; contact the Forest Service before you depart on your trip to learn the fire conditions. Build fires out in the open. Never build a fire against a large rock, because the black scar will remain for centuries. Avoid damp stones when building a fire ring. Wet stones placed around a fire ring can explode dangerously when they become hot. If more than one fire ring exists in a camping area, choose one to use and dismantle the rest, scattering the rocks and half-burned logs. Pack out old aluminum foil and cans that you find in the rings.

Use only fallen wood for fires. Leave the hatchets behind and never cut down any trees. Never make a campfire where downed wood is not extremely plentiful. If there is little firewood around and you must walk a good distance to find any, it is a good indication that the area is overused and that you should not make fires there. Use what's available to start a campfire. Never strip birch bark off a tree for fire starting. Use dry evergreen needles, dry twigs found under the evergreen boughs, dry leaves, and lichens. Make a fuzz stick for a firestarter by shaving slivers on a twig, leaving the shavings attached. Know your woods. Softwoods make quicker kindling but sparks can cause fires; these woods burn out quickly. Stick to hardwoods. Candle stubs are an excellent way to start a fire, especially when firewood is wet. They can sit in the fire tinder for a long time drying out the wood ... much longer than a match. Carry tinder (fire starter) in your pocket during the day to keep it dry if you must rely on a fire to cook your supper and conditions are very wet.

Campfires should be small—make toe warmers, not bonfires. Direct smoke away from yourself. Smoke does not actually follow *you* around the fire. It's attracted to the vacuum formed by a large object, namely your body. If you build a short wall of rocks behind one part of the ring, the smoke will rise in that direction, leaving you on the other side, free to cook, get warm, and enjoy yourself. When you are trying to dry out your clothing and gear by the fire, never place any item closer to the heat than where you can comfortably hold your hand. Make sure fires are out before you retire for the night. Make sure they are cold before you leave camp the next morning.

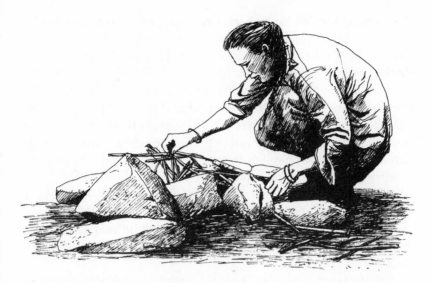

Securing Your Food

Before you retire into your tent for the night, gather all of your food and put it into your stuff sack. It's a good idea to hang it even if you are away from regularly used sites where, you can be sure, critters visit on nightly raids. We at least like to get it off the ground and away from mice and raccoons. The worst night we ever had with small animals occurred on the AT in New Jersey with our darling 4-Hers. The camp van brought cold chicken on the bone up for an evening treat and left us to deal with the remains. We hung it in plastic bags in the trees but the smell drove the local raccoons, which were almost the size of bear cubs, insane. All night long they walked in the woods around the site, crinkling dry leaves and clawing the tree trunks that held the food bags. Our kids were scared to bits, as they slept under open tarps with their flashlights aimed and glued on the pests for the duration of the night.

Mice in the shelters can be another nightmare. You must hang your food sacks and leave all of your pockets open in your pack so they can investigate freely. Coated nylon and closed zippers mean nothing to a hungry mouse. They will chew right through it. Some AT thru-hikers carry traps and one reported a grand total of fifteen in one shelter!

Keeping your food from national park bears is another matter entirely. Black bears (*Ursus americanus*) will eat almost anything—from farm crops to month-dead deer to human food and garbage.

They are opportunistic feeders. Once they develop a taste for human food, they prefer it. They often alter their wild behavior and foraging habits to continue to obtain it. They are smart, and they catch on quickly, learning how to manipulate the devices that were invented to keep them away. When lured into close contact with humans, they lose their special wild and free quality, yet retain their dangerous ability to wound. They begin to beg for food, become "panhandlers," and learn to bluff-charge and chase people to obtain their food. They break into structures, vehicles, or back-country gear where food is improperly stored.

The counterbalance method of food storage described below is the only method of hanging food that will buy you enough time to react. It does not guarantee your food will be safe. Every year, the park bears become more adept at obtaining even properly stored food.

Divide your food and anything with an odor into two stuff sacks. Find a limb about 20 feet from the ground. Throw a rope over the limb, keeping it 10 feet away from the trunk of the tree. Tie one bag to one end of the rope. Pull the sack up to the top of the limb. Reach up as far as you can, and tie the second sack to the rope, also tying up any excess rope. Next, tie a loop a tad longer than the sack, to aid in retrieving the sacks. Before you hoist up this second sack, attach a #2 test monofilament line to your loosely coiled excess line in the event that a suitable long stick to pull with is not available. Toss the lower bag up toward the limb so the top bag drops down to balance it. Push or pull the sacks until they are even; they should be about 12 feet off the ground. With counterbalancing, there's no tie-off rope for an animal to chew.

Sanitation

When we want to teach our 4-H kids something, something that is very important, something we want to stick with them and become part of them, we don't merely just preach the facts, we show them. Along the route that we take them, on the AT in New Jersey, there is a shelter that is heavily used. For a few years running, the outhouse was either filled up at that particular time of the summer, or it was waiting for a new location. Consequently, everyone that visited the area had to dig their own cathole. Merely going for a short walk in the woods, away from the shelter, illustrated the fact that most campers do not know the proper way to dispose of their bodily waste. Behind every tree sat piles of fly-covered turds, with toilet paper stuck into the tops. It was disgusting. The kids were disgusted, and it often takes a lot to disgust a twelve-year-old boy. We were sure they would take the shovel and walk very far into the woods and dispose of theirs properly.

Some folks have a very hard time dealing with this very basic and necessary bodily function in the woods. My first group of 4-H girls refused to go to the bathroom for days. At the end of the second day, some could barely walk. I thought it was ridiculous and so that night, before retiring, I grabbed the flashlight and a roll of toilet paper and marched them all into the woods. I put the beam of light over my work and said, "This is how you do it. It's not such a big deal." Most of them were mortified. I never heard anyone com-

plain again, however, and they all asked for the shovel on a regular basis from then on.

I've taken adults into the woods who had a hard time with it, too. People who have never camped away from park lavatories wonder how it is done. No one talks about it, but they should, because the woods are full of their poor habits.

Choose a location for your hole, well away from creeks, streams, and lakes—200 feet minimum, if possible. Check the area for drainage and gullies, washes, et cetera, where running water could carry it into a water source and contaminate it. Walk at least 150 feet away from any campsite, too. Dig about 6 inches down so animals do not disturb it. Don't bury your toilet paper and don't burn it. Burning was the way to go for some years, but it poses too much of a threat for forest fire. You packed the toilet paper in, you can pack it out. Seal it up tightly in a zip-lock plastic bag. The same goes for tampons, sanitary pads, and diapers. Cover your hole with the soil that you took out and tap it down. If there is a rock nearby, I like to cover the soil with it to prevent animals from being tempted.

If you are winter camping and are spending the night at a designated campsite, one you can be sure will be visited come spring, pack out your fecal matter too. I caretook a shelter on the AT in Pennsylvania for years that had no outhouse. Every March, on my monthly shelter check, I had the disgusting job of picking up the winter campers' piles of toilet paper and piles of turds. Deep snow could have prevented them from digging into the soil, but in the winter, the ground is often too frozen to dig anyway. Packing it out is the best method of disposal.

When urinating, keep away from high-use areas—by trails, campsites, et cetera. Stick to areas of the least visitation. Remember that not disposing of your waste properly is not only disgusting, it contributes to the spread of *Giardia,* a water-borne intestinal parasite.

Litter

When we get our 4-H'ers every summer, we have only about six days to teach them all they need to know about hiking, backpacking, and caring for the earth and their fellow human beings. We have a lot to cover and a lot of competition. One of the biggest hurdles we must get over is getting them not to litter, and then to actually see litter and to pick it up and carry it out. They resist it more than anything else (except quiet time at night). We drill into their heads that nothing, absolutely nothing, gets left behind. Not a single hard-boiled egg shell or orange slice. No one wants to look at their garbage for years while it's waiting to decompose.

. Before we leave a rest spot or campsite, we always make them look behind the rock they are sitting on for wrappers or scraps of food or plastic bags or twisties. We instruct them to pick up trash that they see on the trail as they walk, too—trash that is not theirs or the group's. If someone misses it (or ignores it), the next person can pick it up and make someone else carry it by putting it in his or her pack. A conscientious litter picker-upper need never carry it. We had one young boy who dearly hated to get his hands soiled. He carried his own private stash of individual packets of pre-moistened wipes and used about a half dozen a day. He was *always* busy when it came time to police the campsite before leaving. We asked him continually to help and he wouldn't. So, he was designated to carry the community trash bag on top of his pack, which leaked smelly garbage juice from the holes that the broken beer bottles made in the bag. He wasn't happy about it, but he learned the hard way.

Todd does not get angry easily. When the kids first met him, some cocky souls may even have considered him to be a pushover. One particular group was having problems minding their litter. Todd found a soggy, jelly-soaked white-bread sandwich shoved under the shelter floor once. Then, he found an empty container of cereal. He knew just who it was and confronted him.

"What kind of cereal did you have this morning, Ned?"

Ned answered, "Frosted Flakes," the right answer. (He wasn't smart enough to lie.)

"What did you do with the empty container?"

"It's in my pack."

"Let's see it."

"Oh, it's buried on the bottom. It's too hard to get."

"Get it," Todd said.

Meanwhile, the rest of the kids were wandering over to the shelter, ready to regroup for the day. They stopped dead in their tracks, frightened, when they heard Todd bellow out, "You think I'm stupid?" as he threw the cereal container at Ned, which Todd

had all along in *his* pack. Not a single piece of trash was left behind again. The kids showed so much respect for this gentle man. They laughed later and said that they were afraid Todd was going to eat Ned, he was so mad.

Carry a trash bag and keep it handy. We use an empty bread bag for our own garbage. We smash empty cans flat and have "trash fires" some evenings when conditions are safe and we've accumulated a lot. For short weekend trips, we carry a large garbage bag and pack out others' garbage. If everyone does more than their share, the woods and backcountry will look clean and beautiful, despite a few inconsiderate visitors.

PLAYING IT SAFE

▲ ▲ ▲ ▲ ▲ ▲ ▲ ▲ ▲

C H A P T E R

Dealing with Weather

▲ ▲ ▲ ▲ ▲ ▲ ▲ ▲ ▲

*T*here's no scientific evidence supporting nature's ability to predict the weather for entire seasons. The woolly bear caterpillar's coat is more a fashion statement than a weather prognosticator, and the groundhog's shadow, a media event. Still, nature sometimes gives you hints. Most animals can sense variations in weather a day or two in advance, and they often change their habits accordingly. Likewise, there are general signs in nature an astute human can read. Keep in mind that many of these changes are subtle; you've got to recognize the norm before you can notice a change. So dust off your senses, tune into the following change-in-weather hints, and you'll never again have to rely on the predictably unreliable six o'clock weatherperson.

Natural Signs Indicating Weather

One of the most reliable natural weather indicators is the pine cone. In dry weather, the scales shrivel, open up, and stand out stiffly. When rain is on the way, the scales become pliable and tighten, having absorbed moisture from the air.

When a large number of waterfowl move south in the fall it is a sure sign of bad weather moving in.

All animals are more active in the 24-hour period before a storm. The larger animals such as deer and moose feed heavily, and the smaller animals such as mice scurry to higher ground. All animal activity will usually come to a halt right before the storm begins.

128

When you notice a large number of hawks circling in the sky or perching in the tall tree tops at their "lookouts," a storm is moving in. They are watching the increased activity of the mice and small animals as they move across open ground.

Ants will build tiny "dikes" or mounds at the entrance to their tunnels right before it rains; their activity will cease within an hour of the storm's onset.

When you see squirrels working in front of their homes on a fresh pile of cones, a storm is on the way. The bigger the pile, the longer the storm.

Insect-eating birds feed lower to the ground when a storm is nearing, and higher when the weather is to remain fair. They're simply following the insects, which are forced higher in fair-weather updrafts.

Leaves of deciduous trees will turn bottomside up about 12 to 24 hours before a storm moves in.

Ground smells become much stronger as bad weather moves closer. Muskeg, swamp, marshland, and tideland odors all become more perceptible.

A storm is nearing when the high winds pick up and begin to extend lower and lower to the earth, making the forests roar and the trees bend in submission.

Because water conducts sound more efficiently than air, distant sounds such as grouse drumming, train whistles, owls hooting, and people chopping wood become more audible and distinct when wet weather is coming. The same is true as the air grows colder.

Hemp rope, canvas, and wooden handles all absorb moisture and tighten with the increased dampness in an approaching storm. Your hair will feel thicker and curly hair will become more unruly. Salt will also pick up moisture and begin to swell.

When smoke from your campfire hangs low, a storm is moving in. Smoke rising straight up means clear weather.

Lots of dew or frost on the grass usually means the day will be fair, for it indicates that rain or snow can hardly fall. If dew or frost fails to precipitate come morning, however, conditions favor wet weather.

Morning-glory blossoms open wide when fair weather is on its way, but close up when inclement weather approaches.

Morning mist rising from gorges or ravines is a reliable fair-weather indicator. Any reversal of normal air currents (down the mountain in morning, and up at day's end) is a warning of an approaching storm.

A red-sky sunset means rain within the next 24 hours is unlikely; the color occurs when there is little moisture in the atmosphere. A red sky or red sun at dawn means a storm is approaching.

A corona, or ring, around the moon is caused by the refraction of light through ice crystals in the atmosphere. If the corona increases and expands as the night progresses, it's a sign that rain or snow is on the way.

If the evening sky is overcast and gray, it shows that the dust particles in the air have become so laden with moisture that rain will most likely begin to fall.

Hypothermia

The most common cause of death in the outdoors is exposure to the elements. This leads to hypothermia—the loss of body heat. The victim's core body temperature drops so low (below 95 degrees Fahrenheit), that he or she cannot bring it back up without outside help. Temperatures don't have to be freezing for hypothermia to occur. It results from a combination of air temperature, wind chill, wetness, fatigue, hunger, and exertion. It can occur at any time of the year, and it can happen when everything the victim needs to survive is right by his or her side.

We have a friend in Washington state who is on a search and rescue team. He told us of one particular tragedy where a man who was out hunting in the Cascade Mountains never returned. He must have gotten turned around and became very upset, hiking frantically with no direction. The search and rescue team could not locate his body at the time. Because his widow donated large sums of money to support the team every year, each year thereafter they, in turn, went out for another search to try to locate her husband's remains. A few years later they found him, sitting on a stump, full backpack by his side with clothes, water, matches—everything necessary to sustain life. That is, everything but a calm mind and a sense of reason, one of the symptoms when you experience hypothermia, and what he needed to save his life.

The most obvious case of hypothermia that Todd ever witnessed took place while he was hiking on the AT in the Smoky Mountains of North Carolina. It was a raw day—blowing rain and low temperatures. Todd and his buddies were already set up in the shelter when a couple in their fifties entered. They exchanged hellos. All seemed normal. Then the man went over to the stone fireplace—the *empty* stone fireplace—and began striking matches and throwing them onto the floor. He did this with most of the pack of matches. He said he was going to start a fire to warm himself, yet there was no paper, kindling, or wood. Todd and his friends looked at each other and said, "These folks need help." They got their rain gear off them, instructed them to get into their sleeping bags, and fired up their stoves so they could cook some hot soup for them.

It's difficult to say when exactly the victim becomes more than just cold and at risk of hypothermia and when hypothermia has set in and your intervention is absolutely necessary to sustain his or her life. If a victim manages to shiver and keep awake through the night, he or she can probably get a handle on it come morning if the sun were to come out. It was obvious that these folks' reasoning was impaired. They might not have known enough to get into their sleeping bags, let alone eat, had Todd and his buddies not found them.

We saved two groups from hypothermia on top of 14,495-foot Mount Whitney in the Sierra Nevada of California. Three young backpackers were so tired and hungry and cold that they sat down in the snow to take a nap. Once you sleep, you die, and advanced stages of hypothermia make you very sleepy. We dragged them bodily to the summit shelter, where we did all of the necessary things to bring their body temperatures back up. They insisted they were fine, even the next morning when they had their wits about them. I beg to differ. I think they were quite fortunate that we found them when we did.

The other incident on Mount Whitney was the most interesting and enlightening experience with hikers and hypothermia that we've had. In 1988, Todd and I and our two friends were traversing the 800-mile Sierra Nevada Range. When we climbed Mount Whitney with loaded packs, we were toward the end of our journey and were feeling strong. It was still not an easy thing to accomplish. We still got very fatigued and experienced some light-headedness because of the altitude. The day hikers around us were really suffering. On the summit is a stone shelter that we were spending the night in.

Later that evening, we were sitting on the rocks watching the sunset and that fabulous view when we heard voices down below. Rock climbers were on the face. Time went by, dusk fell, and they were still down there. Their voices were very distinct. They had to be very close. We retired for the night and expected to have some company in the shelter fairly soon. But no one came. Our friend DJ took a walk out to the edge in his flip-flops with his compact flashlight to see if he could learn what was going on. The temperature had dropped to the 20s. Wind chill lowered it to the teens. When he came back to report, he said, "I think they're in trouble. I heard them talking. They're building a stone wall around themselves and are planning on spending the night on the face. They're so close. I could rock-scramble down to where they are."

And so he did; he directed them up without ropes, in his flip-flops, with a tiny flashlight. Once inside, we discovered that they had no sleeping bags, tent, ground cloth, or warm clothes with them. They had a little water and a bit of food. They weren't planning on spending the night up there. In fact, they expected to make it all the way back down to their camp before night fell.

Two members of the party asked if we had climbed up. We said, "Yes, on the John Muir Trail." They replied, "Oh, you only walked up. *We* climbed up the face." We felt small and our accomplishment inadequate.

As the tiny stone room we were sleeping in was packed wall to wall, one of our guys climbed through a hole in the wall to open a window in the next room for the climbers to get in. Over there, they found some pieces of old plastic to cover with. In addition, we sent over our ground cloths and space blankets.

The plastic rattled for a long time and they never quite quieted down. Soon they were calling to us. "We're really cold over here." We told them to join us in our room and we gave them all of our extra clothing and food to eat. They still weren't warming up, so we offered up a sleeping bag and DJ and Todd and I got into one. No one slept a wink all night. Some of them were trying to sleep sitting up. It was very tight in our bag but at least we were warm.

We had 15 miles to hike the next day and many thousands of feet to descend. Every member of our group felt headachy from lack of sleep. When we saw the climbers down in the valley in a pizza shop in town, they didn't even offer to buy us a beer. Perhaps they didn't realize how much danger they were in just the night before. Perhaps their reasoning was impaired and they didn't know enough to be grateful to us for saving their hides.

After all of these incidents and experiences, we feel we really know what hypothermia is and know its symptoms. More importantly, we watch for the conditions that are conducive to hypothermia. We often say, when it's raining a cold 35- to 50-degree rain, "These are prime hypothermia conditions." Then we look out for it. We make sure we rest and eat sufficiently. We make sure we have enough clothes on and the right *kind* of clothes to stay warm and dry.

We can push it then, too—hike in just our rain jackets and bare-skinned legs even though they are red and cold from the melting snow—because we know that we will be in a shelter in a mile or two. We make sure we hike fast enough to keep our body heat up and that the terrain is gentle and easy so we don't get too exhausted. If not, we make sure we stop under some shelter to eat some food and put on rain pants and long underwear to prevent hypothermia from setting in.

Todd and his buddies were pushing it too far when they needed the strength of two hands to press a little toggle switch on their pack to open it. Buttoning a shirt took more than 5 minutes of intense concentration and extreme effort. Part of the problem at this initial stage occurs when you stop to take care of things. The cold and the wind and the rain make you so much colder and quickly because you have suddenly stopped moving and no heat is being produced. As you slowly fumble around, your condition can worsen rapidly. It is important to stop *before* your motor abilities begin to falter. The hard part is knowing before that time comes.

Todd and his friends' destination that hypothermic day was a motel. If they had to set up a tent, they all agreed, they could have been in trouble. They were in the company of other hikers who knew the danger signs and to look out for them. They *knew* what steps to take to alleviate the condition. Educating yourself to know what hypothermia is and how it makes you behave is half the battle. The best thing, however, is to never allow the situation to progress to a dangerous one by taking care of things early.

Treating Hypothermia

Shivering is the first danger sign of hypothermia. It is the body's effort to generate more heat. If outside warmth is not supplied, the victim experiences confusion and sometimes difficulty speaking. Reaction time slows down and judgment is impaired. As heat loss continues, the victim becomes apathetic. Other symptoms include a slower pulse and respiration, a vacant expression, and loss of consciousness. Many victims want to curl up and go to sleep. Death inevitably follows.

Because hypothermia victims commonly become disoriented, they often do not recognize that they are in danger. Therefore, every member of a party should be alert to the signs of the onset of hypothermia in their companions.

If you or your friend begins to shiver, do the following:

- Stop hiking. Get out of the wind and rain. Conserve your energy.
- Administer hot drinks but avoid alcohol, coffee, and tea. These beverages are diuretics, causing loss of body fluid. Alcohol is also a depressant, and the victim should be kept awake at all costs.
- Get the victim out of wet clothes.
- Build a fire or heat warm water.
- Use canteens as hot water bottles.
- If necessary, the victim and a partner should strip naked and get into a dry sleeping bag together. One person's body warmth can save another's life.
- Eat high-energy foods to quickly resupply the body with fuel.

But prevention is the best medicine:

- Wear wool or polypropylene, which insulates even when wet.
- Dress in layers, and regulate your body heat by adding or subtracting garments as necessary.
- Eat high-protein, high-energy foods regularly.
- Drink plenty of fluids, including an occasional hot drink. Diets rich in protein require more fluid to digest than do diets rich in carbohydrates.
- Stay dry. Be prepared for rain even if clear skies are forecasted.
- Wear a hat. Most body heat is lost through the head.
- Most importantly, don't underestimate the chance of hypothermia or overestimate your endurance or that of your companions.

Hints and Tips for Rain

Take care of things before they get extreme. Eat before you get very hungry. Rest before you get very tired. Put on warm clothes before you are freezing. And remember to look out for each other because one of the early signs of hypothermia is not thinking clearly.

Do not put your spare dry clothes on come morning if rain the previous day made what you were wearing wet. You will need those dry clothes come evening, when your activity has ceased and you need to be warm. As uncomfortable as it feels, put the wet clothes back on. After a few minutes of exercise, they will warm up from your body heat and dry as time goes by. If you are in danger of hypothermia, however, take the wet clothes off immediately.

The same goes for socks. Grit your teeth and slide the wet fabric over your feet. The moisture will become less noticeable within minutes and they too will dry before your first break. Throughout the course of a rainy day, take your boots off occasionally to wring out your wet socks. Refrain from putting dry ones on because they will quickly become wet. The newly wrung-out socks will feel remarkably more comfortable.

Most rain jackets do not come with a substantial enough hood for keeping rain off your eyeglasses. Hook a baseball hat or visor onto the outside of your pack for such circumstances and wear it alone or under your hood. The visor will keep your head much cooler.

A fanny pack worn in the front is a very important piece of equipment when backpacking in the rain. Pack some high-energy snacks before you leave in the morning and a bottle of water if space allows, so you will not be tempted to skip those necessary breaks to refuel. Not only will you feel stronger as you hike in inclement weather—a time when a hiker's energy usually functions at a low—but you will safeguard yourself from becoming hypothermic as well.

Grab the opportunity to rest when you come across a dry area—a porch on a trailside cabin, an overhanging rock, a thick stand of evergreens, even a dry culvert. If the sky is threatening but rain has not begun to fall, rest and snack before you feel you need to, in case you will not be able to stop in the near future. That way, once it begins to rain, you will be well rested and well nourished.

Wearing full rain gear is not necessary in a light, warm summer rain. You should protect your backpack with its rain cover as soon as it begins to precipitate, but you may be able to hold off putting on your own rain gear. Your pack will offer adequate protection for your torso, where your vital, heat-producing organs are. As the rain increases or the temperature drops, your situation changes from damp/dry and comfortably cool to wet and possibly hypothermic. Put your rain gear on long before you reach the danger zone.

If you are wearing cotton clothing underneath your rain garments, it could be making you colder rather than warmer. Wet cotton not only feels cold, it can *cause* hypothermia. Better to take it off and wear nothing underneath, if you are comfortable with this. If the temperature is really cold, wear polypropylene long underwear underneath your rain gear.

Always carry enough clothing for the worst possible weather for the time of year that you are hiking in. Don't rely on the weather forecaster's favorable report.

Keep clean plastic bags in your rain-jacket pockets to use as gloves when the rain is a cold one. The thin produce bags found in grocery stores work well. The bag/gloves enable you to open your fingers to grasp things like a hiking staff or an ice axe. It can pour rain or snow a blizzard and your hands can stay out of your pockets and remain warm and dry. The bags behave like a vapor barrier, only allowing your hands to sweat to a point. One October, while we hiked in the rainy Cascades of Washington, I was in bad need of some gloves. I had lost one bread bag out of my pocket. The only spare was our garbage bread bag whose contents we had just emptied into a receptacle in town. It stank terribly from the sardine can and onion skins that were in it and made my hands smell for days afterward, but it was better than having my fingers freeze.

Hints and Tips for Cold

Pacing yourself is important in winter activities to prevent exhaustion and to stay warm. Always match your pace to your breathing, never your breathing to your pace.

Never sleep in the clothes you have worn all day. They will be damp and be poor insulators, even if they do not feel damp to the touch. Keep an extra pair of long underwear just for sleeping in, perhaps inside your sleeping bag. Sleeping nude is better than sleeping in damp clothes. A spare pair of sleeping socks is a good idea also.

If you are cold upon awakening, don't quickly get out of your bag and run around in the cold. First, do some isometrics, like pushing your palms together, to raise your body temperature and warm yourself before unzipping your bag and losing your insulated heat.

If your feet are freezing in your sleeping bag at night, slide your bag's stuff sack over your bag's foot for greater insulation.

Try to keep your nose and mouth out of your sleeping bag so it doesn't absorb water from your breath. (One quart of water per night is lost this way.) Also, keep your wet clothes out of your sleeping bag. If you want to dry them, try laying them in between your sleeping pad and the tent floor. They will dry somewhat and, at least, not freeze.

Don't put another pair of socks on if there is not sufficient room in your boots for it. Your tight, constricted toes will be colder with the extra socks on. And remember that your feet usually swell an entire size larger when carrying weight on your back.

Lightning

When we hiked over the John Muir Trail one summer, we had some very strange weather. It was almost like we were hoaxed. I had read enough of John Muir's writings to know that cumulus clouds often built up in the afternoon, bringing on a late, short shower. Nearly every day that we traveled the high country, we were hit with a thunder-and-lightning storm—*just* as we were going over the pass. It didn't matter what time of day we went over the pass, either— noon, 2:00 P.M., 4:00 P.M., 7:00 P.M. One night we camped 2 miles below Forrester Pass, at 13,000 feet the highest pass on the John Muir Trail. We wanted to get up and over it before the clouds built up. As unbelievable as it sounds, by the time we arrived at the highest point of the pass, the thunder was booming! And it was in the middle of the morning! We crossed nearly every pass on that trail in a hurried or even a frantic fashion because of the storms.

The backcountry rangers are afraid of lightning. When I heard that, I knew my own personal fears were not so foolish. Up there, you have to sometimes go 6 or 8 miles before you can get under cover—sparse, scrubby trees at that. That's a long time to run with a full pack. When we reached Mather Pass, we were getting tired of not being able to rest, refuel, and enjoy the views the High Sierra had to offer. We had just dumped our lunch bags onto our foam pads and were getting ready for a nice break when the thunder started rolling. We quickly stuffed the food back into the sacks and begrudgingly shouldered our packs. Our friend, Heath, however, had had enough.

"I'm staying right here and enjoying my peanut butter sandwich," he said.

"Pack up if it starts to lightning," I told him. Partway down the granite wall, lightning cracked from nowhere, directly over our heads. We all jumped into the air. *Holy shit!* That was close! We all looked up to see if Heath was coming and, sure enough, he had packed up in seconds flat and was running back and forth down the tight switchbacks, like a ball in a pinball machine or a marble in a zigzag marble roll.

"All I could think of," he said, out of breath, when he caught up to us, "was what I would do with three dead people up here."

"*You* were the one in the most danger," we told him, "standing on the pass like a lightning rod."

When you are climbing up to an exposed ridge or summit and thunder is rolling around, there is that big question to consider—should we continue going *upward?* Perhaps the storm won't even come over this peak. It may be difficult to see what direction it's moving from where you are. Perhaps you can get up and over before it even arrives. Do you hurry like mad and try to beat it? You feel awfully foolish continuing upward when the sky is black and crackling. Do you sit and stay put where you are? It could take hours for the storm to pass and may not even be necessary to stop. Besides, where you are may not be the safest spot, either. We usually try to go for it if we are close at all. Adrenaline is surging

and any discomfort like a blister or a sore knee or hunger or thirst or even fatigue is totally swept aside in your mind while you just concentrate on getting over and down.

"Middle ground" is supposed to be safest. We always have a difficult time determining what is the "middle." Halfway down to the valley from the summit? What if the trail remains on the ridge for awhile? Do you abandon it and go cross-country over the side to get down low? Several hundred yards off the peak is probably much safer.

There are some easy precautions to keep in mind that don't take a lot of decision making. Avoid prominent objects like the tallest tree or boulder. Lightning could be attracted to it. If you are the most prominent object on the landscape, assume a crouched position with both feet together. Keep the rest of your body off the ground, away from your packframe, knife, et cetera, and away from your comrades by about 8 feet. Overhanging cliffs and small caves should be avoided, for lightning can come down and jump across the edge and pass through your body.

Hyperthermia

I've gotten the initial stages of hyperthermia often while hiking in the hot, humid Mid-Atlantic states. Much of the summer you can feel like a wet dishrag while you hike, because the sweat cannot evaporate from your skin because there is too much moisture in the air. My head would ache, my face would be beet red and very hot. Trying to climb in the heat of the day always did it to me, especially in open areas where the sun can beat down on you.

Hiking in the desert of California has made me feel the same way, minus the humidity. There was often no shade to cool down beneath—only small scrub sage bushes where you literally had to lie on the ground to get in their shade, and I did.

Our friends were sending us salt-free snacks at that point in our trip. It made us laugh. Perhaps at home they were concerned with too much salt in their diet, but our concern was the opposite on that desert trail. We craved it, and began leaving town stops with a bag of nacho chips. We'd lick the salty seasoning from our fingers, drink some water, and feel like new human beings. There were times when we opened our plastic container of salt and dipped our moistened fingers into it and then popped them into our mouths. Within minutes, we felt better. Todd used to send about one-eighth of a cup of salt with his supplies to every town stop. Before I met him, I never carried it and, I must admit, since I began using it, I can perform so much better in the heat.

You can drink all the water that you want, but you must also take in salt, electrolytes, and food to keep the water in your body. If not, it will flow right through you when you urinate.

When it comes to carrying water and covering miles to get to your next water source, it is always a toss-up: Should you carry two gallons in your water bag? This will make you so weighted down that you become very fatigued and need to rest often, thereby taking more time to get to your next source, maybe even necessitating spending the night, which really demands a lot of water. Or do you carry much less than you'll desire and hope to cover the miles quicker and alleviate a night in the woods and the need for more water? Both alternatives are painful. When we hiked in northern California on the Pacific Crest Trail, we opted for a death march into Burney Falls State Park, 21 miles away. After lunch, we had 14 miles remaining. At the first few breaks, a pint slid down easily. Then we began rationing. We split the remaining mileage into five sections. On each of our four breaks, we were allowed one-fourth of our remaining water. We looked at our watch constantly, throughout the afternoon, and collapsed at the mileage point for the next break, groping for the side pocket that held the precious liquid. It was rough, but we were very happy when we got to the inexhaustible supply of liquid at the end of the day.

Consuming adequate amounts of water and salt is one of your best safeguards for preventing heat exhaustion and hyperthermia. Like hypothermia, there is a fine line between pushing your body and going into the danger zone. Had we felt much more hot than thirsty that day outside Burney, we would have decided on another plan, like staying put during the day and covering the miles at night by flashlight, when the thirst-stealing sun is no longer out. Night hiking, especially in snake country, produces its own threats, but in that situation, it might have been the lesser evil.

Treating Hyperthermia

When the body's cooling system becomes strained and it cannot regulate itself, the result is **heat exhaustion**. The victim can become pale with shallow breathing. He or she may complain of nausea, headache, and dizziness. His or her pupils may dilate and vomiting may occur. Move the victim to a cool, shady spot, loosen his or her clothing, raise his or her feet, apply cool, wet cloths, and have him or her drink sips of water.

When the body's cooling system breaks down completely, the result is **heat stroke** and it is a life-or-death matter. The victim's face will be hot, and his or her body could be dry. His or her pupils will be very small. He or she will have a rapid, strong pulse, will breathe slowly and noisily, and perhaps be unconscious. Lay the victim on his or her back with his or her head and shoulders elevated. Remove clothing and cover him or her with dripping-wet cloths and towels, especially his or her head. Continually douse with water and be ready to administer mouth-to-mouth resuscitation at any time. Seek medical assistance at once.

To guard against hyperthermia:

- Consume plenty of water; on hot days, your body can lose about two quarts an hour.
- Wear light-colored clothing to reflect the heat.
- Cotton will wick moisture from the skin and the evaporation will help keep you cooler.
- Wear sunglasses.
- A hat with a brim will help shade your head.
- Dipping your head in a cool stream will refresh you and keep you cooler as the water evaporates from your skin.
- When you feel too warm, rest in the shade.
- When the temperature soars, ease up on strenuous exercise.

Hints and Tips for Heat

Before you go out on a hot-weather backpack, condition yourself by working up a full body sweat five times a week a month ahead of time. By doing this, you will build heat tolerance by consistently raising the body's internal temperature.

Suntan lotion can interfere with the body's ability to cool itself by preventing perspiration from evaporating. It is better to cover your body with the right type of clothing or at least not to apply the lotion generously.

In extreme heat, your appetite will diminish and you may find fatty foods unappealing. This may be because they take more oxygen to burn than other foods and it is your body's way of compensating. Make sure you have a variety of foods to choose from.

Cooling the top of your head will have a cooling effect on your entire body. Soak your head and shirt in streams and rivers every chance you get, especially before a climb. Carry a bandanna to dip into every creek you cross for constant dabbing of your forehead and neck. The temperature of the body is greatly affected by the temperature of the extremities.

If you are traveling in a mountainous region that has lingering snowpatches, stuff your bandanna full of snow and tie two ends under your chin for long-term cooling, or fill a hat with snow. If you are wearing a regular hat, make sure the crown is pushed all the way up to form a pocket of air to insulate your head from the sun's rays.

Reduce talking to conserve your body's water and breathe with your mouth closed. Holding a small pebble in your mouth will cause saliva to be produced and will help to keep your mouth moist.

Walk in the early and late hours of the day when the sun is the lowest and the heat less intense. Use the hottest part of the day for a long rest and siesta, preferably by a water source. You may want to cook your supper meal at this time so you do not have to prepare a hot meal in the dark after your evening miles. Reversing meals, having lunch at night, also prevents you from carrying large quantities of water for the overnight if your camp is dry.

Carry salt and potassium-rich snacks, drinks, and meals, such as dried bananas, apricots, carrots, corn, raisins, chocolate, nuts, crackers, peanuts, peanut butter, and salted seeds to replace your body's electrolytes.

CHAPTER 7

Water

▲ ▲ ▲ ▲ ▲ ▲ ▲ ▲ ▲

*W*ater is very important to life. You can go two weeks without food but only about two days without any water. There is nothing like not having something in your life to make you realize how important it is—not just to your well-being, but to your happiness as well.

When you're backpacking for any length of time, water becomes very important to you—for drinking, for bathing, for cooling off, for recreational swimming, for washing clothes and dishes. Often water is also a natural obstacle to be gotten around or through. At the same time that a stream is a welcome sight to a thirsty hiker, it can often be a cause for trepidation, too, when you see that the trail resumes on the other side of a wide, raging torrent.

Drinking Water

We were on top of the Hat Creek Rim in northern California on the Pacific Crest Trail. It was 7:00 P.M. The sun was still high in the sky with plenty of mileage in it, but our day was over. We arrived at our planned destination on schedule—a reservoir on the plateau. The guidebook encourages you to enjoy a swim and then suggests you camp. As we were without a water source all day, it seemed like good advice to take. The day had been a hot, dry, dusty one. Sweat had dried on my face, making it feel like I had applied a pore-tightening mask. When I rubbed it, salt crystals fell off. We wanted cool, clean water for more than our thirst. I wanted to dunk my head and entire body in it.

When we saw the blue lake below us, shimmering in the sunlight, we ran like crazed cattle down the trail, kicking up dust as we went. At the edge, we stopped dead. The water level was very, very low, exposing rocks and mucky slime all along its shore. In between the rocks was cow manure and billions of breeding mosquitoes. We shooed the cattle away from the edge. Nix the swim, but can we even drink the slop? We had to strain the water through a bandana (while the mosquitos had a meal of our legs) boil it, and treat it with iodine before we felt comfortable drinking it. Ninety-eight degrees at 7:00 in the evening, waiting for boiling-hot iodine water to cool off so we could quench our thirst ... not exactly what we had had in mind.

A water source may not always be what you expect. It may not be like the guidebook says it is, either. It may not even be there.

We left Castle Crags State Park, California, in the heat of the day. High noon to be exact, carrying a pack full of heavy supplies. We stopped often to rest and, because of it, lost track of our mileage and the passing time. All the seasonal creeks were running, so surely the "reliable stream" we were planning on camping at would be, too. Close to the time we were due to arrive there, we crossed a wide, bone-dry creekbed. This couldn't be it. Todd thought we hadn't come quite far enough and so we continued climbing higher while the sun sank lower in the sky. Eight o'clock arrived and still no creek. I was exhausted and famished. We stopped to regroup.

Should we backtrack to the water that was *before* the dry creek bed—6 miles below? Should we try to hold out to the next water source 14 miles ahead? Should we try to continue hiking in the cool of the night? None of the options appealed to us. We noticed that to our side was a steep, narrow gorge. Once we stopped talking, it sounded like water was running through it. Or was it the wind? Wasn't that the same gorge that the dry creekbed was in that we crossed earlier? Perhaps the stream had disappeared underground. Todd decided to take his climbing rope and descend. I stood on the rim, watched, and prayed for his safety. On the climb out, he set off a boulder slide and I lived a moment of hell until I screamed his name and he answered me. Once again, we had our water for the night, but it was not obtained how we expected to obtain it. These episodes have taught us to be prepared and to learn to problem-solve.

As a rule, we don't carry a lot of water in our packs when we hike, unless we know there is a dry stretch ahead. Our water-carrying capacity is always two one-liter bottles apiece and one two-and-a-half-gallon collapsible bladder bag between us for in camp or on very dry stretches. As long as there is water every 4 to 6 miles, we "camel up" and hydrate ourselves, drinking as much as we comfortably can. Then we don't need as much in between sources. We met some hikers in the Desolation Lakes Wilderness in California, an area abundant in water, carrying open gallon milk jugs full of water in their hands. They took sips frequently as they climbed. It looked terribly uncomfortable and, with plentiful water, it was really unnecessary.

It is very important to know the water situation on the trail you will be following. Flow varies from year to year, season to season, even week to week. If you can't learn this information before you leave, be prepared to carry more until you know what the conditions are. We've carried two and a half gallons on our backs (that's twenty extra pounds!) because it was that dry ahead. To figure how much you'll need, and if you're certain there is no water ahead, estimate four quarts per person per day in the heat (less if it's cooler out). We like to have one quart per person overnight. And then you'll need enough to get you to the next water source come morning, depending on how far away it is.

We never completely empty our water bottles, no matter how thirsty we are, until we get to the next source. Then, if it happens to be dry, as in the Castle Crags episode, at least we have some left to carry us through. Taking sips frequently instead of long gulps is best in this type of situation.

Every time you take a break, you should drink some water. Every hour is not too frequent, if you stop every hour. Use your urine color as an indicator of whether or not you are getting adequate fluids. If it is a bit darker than usual, you probably are not drinking enough water. An occasional drink mix is good for helping you to get more fluids into your body, if the water is unappetizing and there is fear of dehydration because of your lack of interest.

We often get dehydrated, to some degree, on the trail. More so in the cold, when we forget to drink, since we don't feel as hot or sweat as much. We actually get dehydrated a little bit every day, for we always drink many quarts in camp once the day is over. That's why you sometimes wake up with "cotton mouth" in the middle of the night. Always keep a bottle handy when you go to sleep for middle-of-the-night sips.

Water Hints and Tips

It is very important to drink water on a regular schedule, not just when you become thirsty, because you do not actually feel thirsty until your body is 20 percent dehydrated. When engaging in prolonged and strenuous activity, drink about a pint every half hour. In hot weather, you should be 100 percent hydrated so your internal body temperature can remain near 99 degrees Fahrenheit.

Be aware that fatigue can disguise thirst and make drinking

seem like too much trouble, when your tired body needs fluid more than ever.

If it's available, always drink more than you feel you really need.

If you don't like to bother taking your pack off to get a drink, rig up a hose leading from your water bottle in your pack's side pocket. Tubing purchased at a surgical supply store or a hardware store works well and can be clamped off and hooked onto your pack's frame when you're not sipping.

As we said earlier, wide-mouth nalgene bottles are the best for carrying water. They make cleaning the bottom easy, where bacteria can grow. They are easy to fill in a stream or spring compared to narrow-mouth bottles. They make a great instant pudding container—easy to fill, shake, and clean. A spoon fits nicely into the wide opening. It is easier to get partially frozen water out. You can also see how much water is left compared to colored bottles or canteens.

Be careful to keep the threads clean on your bottle. Mold and bacteria can easily build up here, especially if you use your bottles for sugary drinks, making dysentery a possibility.

Desert hiking forces you to become super-sensitive to your water needs, because in the dry air, sweat evaporates as rapidly as it is formed, keeping the skin virtually dry and the hiker almost unaware that his or her sweat glands are active, when, indeed, during a really hot day in the desert, his or her body may produce an average of one liter of sweat per hour!

Carrying your water bottle inside your pack in a sock or wrapped in an article of clothing will keep your water much cooler when hiking in hot weather. The night before going on a day hike, freeze the liquid in your water bottle, or at least add some ice before heading out.

In the cold, a hiker who doesn't sweat excessively is often unaware that he or she is losing body fluids. The resulting dehydration seriously impairs the heat-producing capabilities of the body. Drink fluids as often as possible during the day and keep a bottle close by at night.

If you must eat snow (never ice), melt it and warm it in your mouth before swallowing. It will prevent your mouth from drying out and prevent your stomach from chilling.

Fill your partially filled water bottle with snow to stretch your water when traveling on a trail void of water sources. The movement of your hiking will quickly turn the snow to water.

Attach a cord to your water bottle so you can toss it into a creek or lake without getting your hands wet or getting dangerously close to unstable snowbanked edges. Whenever possible, get water from unfrozen sources instead of melting snow.

Turn your water bottles upside down to prevent them from freezing up. (Wide-mouth bottles work best in winter.) Ice will form on the bottom instead, leaving the threads free. If it's very cold, you can sleep with them too. Just make sure your lids are very tight and leakproof.

A wool sock pulled over your bottle will give it some protection from the cold.

Winter hikers need a minimum of three to four quarts of liquid per day.

When melting snow for water during winter camping, always have an inch or so or of starter water in the pan, if possible, then slowly add snow. Use the wettest snow available or icy, crusty snow.

A lidded pot of water buried a foot or so under the snow in a well-marked spot will remain unfrozen overnight because snow is such a good insulator. If you plan to camp in one place for several nights, it is probably better to bury the pot in different locations because snowmelt around the pot produces ice, which is a poor insulator.

Be wary of pink or yellow snow. Watermelon snow gets its name from the color, taste, and scent caused by microorganisms that can bring on diarrhea.

Purifying Water

Fifteen million Americans are infected with *Giardia lamblia* each year from drinking contaminated water. It is a microscopic organism that attaches itself to your small intestine, making you feel bloated and crampy, have diarrhea, and vomit. The symptoms can go on for weeks, months, even years, if left untreated. Prescription medication is the only way to rid your body of these miserable organisms. *Giardia* cysts are carried in the feces of humans and some animals. Purifying your water is the only way to prevent becoming infected.

The three methods of purification are boiling, adding chemical disinfectants, and filtration.

Boiling is the most effective way to purify water but it is the least convenient. Water must be boiled for 5 to 10 minutes, depending on the elevation, then cooled down before it can be drunk. It also uses a lot of precious fuel and time. This method is very impractical for short trips or day hikes.

Using **iodine crystals** or tablets is convenient, easy, lightweight, and inexpensive. As long as you follow the instructions and wait the allotted time, the water-borne "pests" will be killed. Iodine is extremely potent and can be harmful if directions aren't followed carefully, and the resulting flavor of the water leaves a lot to be desired.

Water-purifying **filters** usually consist of a pump that forces water through a ceramic filter for instant purification. Filters with pores .2 microns or smaller are extremely effective in removing *Giardia*. There is no aftertaste in the water and most pump about one liter in 1 to 2 minutes. Filters can be bulky and expensive (weighing between six and twenty-three ounces and costing between $25 and $235), and care must be taken to clean and declog or replace some filters to continue their performance.

When water filters first arrived on the outdoor scene, Todd was not anxious to purchase and carry one. It seemed like a lot of unnecessary weight compared to a bottle of iodine crystals. But we had had our fill of drinking iodized water. Although flavored drink mixes can disguise the disgusting flavor, I don't enjoy the sugar burn-out you sometimes experience afterwards, to say nothing of the weight of those heavy packets (all empty calories), and the fact that mold and bacteria can grow on your bottle, making you sick. We didn't want to chance it and do nothing. That is foolish and the thought of abandoning a long-awaited trip because of giardiasis didn't seem worth it. The water filter was looking better all the time.

Although we nearly always carry a water filter now, Todd goes to great lengths to find where the water comes out of the ground—to the spring. Some hikers still purify even here. Everyone draws the line at different places. Once you've been infected with *Giardia lamblia*, our unfortunate friends have told us, you purify everything that goes into your mouth. Sometimes we think we are immune to it, because of all the unfiltered water we've drunk in our hiking lives; that perhaps it's even in our systems and it doesn't affect us. Someday our tune may change.

There are still some hikers who purify nothing, or purify selectively. Here are some things to keep in mind if you are in that

group. Never drink standing water or water that flows through cow country. Always go to the source if you can possibly find it and it's not too far away or inaccessible. Take it where it is running, over a rock, for example, instead of where it eddies back into a still pool. Study your map: Are there houses or civilization above your source? Does it run through pastureland? Come out of a lake? Has it traveled a long distance above ground or has it just surfaced a quarter mile up the hollow? A dead raccoon could be lying in the stream out of sight just above you and you'll never know it. Something like that is always a possibility. If you find yourself on the trail without sufficient water from home and without means of purifying it, by being very selective of where you obtain it, you should narrow your chances of becoming ill from contaminated water.

Washing/Bathing

For a number of years, New Jersey's 4-H program hired us to take their eleven- and twelve-year-olds out on a summer week-long backpacking trip. It coincided with that particular county's summer camp, for that age group proved to be difficult in a regimented camp situation. They were not always a breeze to deal with on the trail, either. One of our most embarrassing experiences was over a spring on the AT. We were camping by a shelter, in the part of the summer when the wave of thru-hikers is in the area, too. Todd and I instructed our kids on proper water treatment and trail ethics. We were shocked and infuriated when an upset seventy-year-old long-distance hiker came to us complaining about our kids. He had just pulled into camp after a 20-mile day and was very tired and thirsty. When he went to the spring, which was barely running, three of our boys were sitting there laughing and *soaking their feet!* right in the pool where it comes out of the ground!

"Who's responsible for these kids?" he yelled. "Can't you keep them under control?" Todd and I were so upset. They knew perfectly well not to do such a thing. Fortunately, because we knew that the spring would be slow in that dry time of the year, we had arranged with the camp to drop off a ten-gallon container of water. We made the boys offer it to the hiker first and then invite him to dinner, which was quite a spread, and apologize profusely. We also told them to tell the hiker that they were taught proper trail ethics but did not listen.

I have often seen particles of food on the bottom of a spring's pool, left over from a camper washing his or her dishes. "It's bio-degradable," they rationalize. So are some soaps, but why would you want to drink it or eat it or see someone's garbage floating in it?

Never put anything into a water source that could pollute it. Keep all soap at least 200 feet away from any stream, lake, or spring. To wash your dishes, fill a basin or pot with water, carry it away from the source, wash your dishes, and then scatter it. Go back to the source to refill it if necessary.

You can wash your entire body this way, too. Take your full pot 50 feet away. Wet your upper body by dipping your bandanna into the pot and swabbing yourself. Soap down, if you desire, then swab yourself again. Toss and refill as needed. When the weather is chilly, you can keep your upper body clothed while washing your lower half and stay relatively chill-free. You can wash your hair this way, too. Some bladder water bags are dark colored and come with a hose to use as a shower. They are placed in the sun to warm the water and then hung in a tree to use.

I've met hikers who washed up every single night, shaved, and put on their clean, in-camp clothes. Others tried to set records for the longest stretch without bathing. It's not very offensive while on the trail in the outdoors. All you have to do is put a hiker and his or her pack in an enclosed area, like a car, however, and most people can't get their windows down quick enough and get the car moving fast enough to force out the bad air. Your body isn't the only thing that is giving off an odor. Pack straps, hip belts, sleeping bags, clothes, all get permeated with sweat and body oils.

When it's warm out, we try to wash up most nights before going to bed. Even a quick water rinse gets the sweat off and prevents you from feeling sticky and dirty. Even bathing a few choice spots like your face, neck, armpits, and genitals is better than nothing. It is also good prevention of rashes and chafing, which can make your hike very uncomfortable. I've seen a number of boils result from a pore getting clogged with dirt and oils. They can be very painful, especially if they are located at a friction spot, like your pack strap or hip belt.

We carry biodegradable soap in a tiny plastic bottle—the kind that had travel-size shampoo or skin lotion in it, and is sold in some drug stores. Some biodegradable soap is so concentrated that a little goes a very long way. Peppermint is our favorite because it smells so fresh, it gives the illusion of being clean, even if you're not.

Stream Fords

A few years back, there was a middle-aged couple who were hiking the entire AT. They were nearing their goal in Maine when they came to the 200-yard-wide Kennebec River, the most famous and formidable ford on the entire trail. It has a swift, powerful current and its depth varies greatly, because the river is used for hydroelectric power. There is no set schedule for the release of the dam waters; it happens automatically when power is needed. (Years ago, you also had to dodge logs as they were floated down the river to the mill.) Up until 1985, most thru-hikers forded the river. George and Alice Ference knew about the map and the diagram that was drawn up and posted in the last trailside shelter before the river. It had diagrams of sandbars and dotted lines showing you exactly where to cross. That same year, however, there had been lots of heavy rains and flooding and the sandbars had moved. The map was of no help. A tragic thing happened to Alice. She was swept away and drowned.

There is no bridge spanning the river. For many years there was a ferryman who would row you safely across for a fee, and with prior notice. However, by the time most thru-hikers reach this part of the trail, their funds are dwindling and the ford is one place to save money. And many hikers see the crossing as one of the greatest challenges of the trail, or at least they did before 1985. But because of Alice's death, the Appalachian Trail Conference and the Maine Appalachian Trail Conference now pay for the ferry service, which is free to hikers. Now, no hiker has to risk the ford unless they so choose.

There are many unbridged fords on the Pacific Crest Trail. Some were raging torrents only during spring runoff when the snow was melting. Other fords had bridges, but they were periodically washed out. One particular section of the guidebook spoke repeatedly of "formidable fords." It made our skin crawl to think of what could be ahead. We grew to hate the word "formidable."

When you first come to a ford, do not think that, because the trail deposited you on this part of the bank, this is where you are supposed to cross. You should ford a stream at the safest spot, not the most convenient. Study the stream up and down to see where others have crossed it in the past.

Sometimes rocks are placed a reasonable distance apart and are large enough and stable enough to hop across on. Remember that your pack will throw off your balance, especially if the rocks are slippery.

Logs may bridge the stream, but if a log is so close to the water that the spray makes it slippery or wet, or if there are many projecting branches to catch your pack, don't walk across it. If the log is safe, carefully consider the stream below. Will you drop far if you fall? Are there jagged rocks or boulders beneath? A long stick or pole can be of considerable help when crossing a log. Place it on the downstream side of the log and lean into it a bit as you cross. This way, if you should fall, you won't be swept against the log and trapped. If you feel uncomfortable on the log, wade the stream instead.

If the stream looks too dangerous to wade and a felled tree is the only way across, you may consider crossing it on your rump. Your legs will hang to the sides and you'll use your hands as leverage. It takes some time to cross this way and it may feel uncomfortable, but it is one of the safest ways to get to the other side.

It can be very dangerous to cross a substantial stream without shoes to protect your feet and prevent slipping. On the PCT, we carried very lightweight sneakers as our in-camp shoes. They were used not only for town walking, but as our fording shoes as well. They helped us keep our boots dry. Some trail stretches had so many new "streams" from snow runoff that we kept them on all day and carried our boots. If you must cross in your boots, take them off to remove your socks and then put them back on barefooted.

Before crossing any substantial stream, loosen your shoulder straps and unbuckle your hip belt. This will enable you to slip out of your pack should you need to abandon it. Lost gear is better than drowning. Take off your excessive clothing if the weather is warm to reduce dragging in swift currents. In cold weather, close-fitting long underwear will help keep you warm. Look for a walking stick on the shore if you don't carry one.

Inexperienced members of your group would do better with assistance. Perhaps take their packs for them. A taut rope stretched across the stream may be useful as a handline, but tying into a rope (belaying) is not recommended; it is possible that the rope could hold the crosser underwater in the event of entanglement or a fall. On potentially dangerous fords, I personally like to cross

with my husband's strong, steady hand in mine.

Here are some things to consider before selecting your crossing point:

- Generally, at a stream's narrow point, it will be the swiftest. The wider parts may be deeper, but they will be easier to wade across.

- Do not walk directly across a stream but angle downstream to the opposite bank.

- Take each step slowly and deliberately. The forward foot should be firmly planted before moving the rear foot. Never hurry.

CHAPTER 8

First Aid

▲ ▲ ▲ ▲ ▲ ▲ ▲ ▲ ▲

*T*he farther Todd progressed on the AT, the more the contents of his first aid kit diminished and deteriorated. In Maine, at the end of the trail, it consisted of his toilet paper for bandages and electrical tape from his repair kit. He started out with much more, but sent some of its content home at every town stop. I was horrified when I learned this and announced that our new hiking partnership would travel with a substantial kit and I would be glad to carry it myself. You can buy a prepackaged first aid kit or put your own together. The content will vary from individual to individual, and depend upon the kind of trip, its length, et cetera. Here are some basic ingredients:

- Half dozen Band-Aids
- Sterile 3-inch gauze pads
- A few butterfly bandages
- Adhesive tape
- Non-aspirin pain reliever
- Needle—for removing splinters/opening blisters
- Antibiotic ointment—half-ounce tube
- Elastic bandage

You may also include an extractor kit (found in some sporting goods stores), which sucks body fluids out of your pores when stung by a bee, et cetera. Todd and I were amazed at how well this works. He often feels light-headed and dizzy after getting stung but with the extractor, he experienced no side effects whatsoever. The kit has no expiration date, contains no medicine, and is very light-weight and inexpensive.

On long trips, you may want to bring along a few prescription drugs like Lomotil for dysentery, or an antibiotic for general infection resulting from injury or illness. If you are severely allergic, you may want an allergy suppressant or if you are prone to urinary tract infections, something to relieve it. Perhaps some first-aid information on what steps to take in various emergency situations would be a good addition, too. A double zip-lock plastic bag is an adequate first aid case.

Blisters

When Todd and I went on his first backpacking trip, he was a senior in high school and it was right before graduation. His feet got soaked in cotton tube socks and his leather work boots were too small. There was a piece of metal sticking out on the inside that jabbed his foot. He got six to eight blisters on each foot; he got blisters where you usually don't usually even get them—between the toes, under the nails—besides the usual spots like on the back of the heel. They went through a few layers of skin, bled, and oozed pus. He had to go to the doctor and take antibiotics. No shoes could touch his feet for several weeks. Then, only modified flip flops (one strap was cut off) were suitable for his graduation footwear.

It's a good thing he truly enjoyed the sport, because with blisters like that, he could have easily decided it wasn't worth it. When your feet feel achy and sour, it somehow feels like your whole body is, too. Since your feet are very important to hiking—they're what propel you over the trail—it's really worth the time to take care of them.

The first sign of blisters developing will be a hot and tender spot on your foot. Now is the time to treat it. Apply moleskin as a preventive measure before a blister even develops. We like moleskin, not molefoam, which is thicker. If a blister isn't infected, or if it's only a hot spot, we put the moleskin on and leave it on.

If you get a blister that is large and quite painful, it may be a good idea to drain it. Wash it first with soap and water. Puncture the skin, at the bottom so it can drain, with a sterilized needle. Use an antibiotic cream to prevent infection. Cover it with a Band-Aid or other nonstick bandage, and then apply moleskin on top. If your blisters are sore and infected, you will need to take your bandage off to clean the wound and reapply it, so you don't want to apply moleskin right on the blister. Some hikers like to cut a round donut hole in the molefoam before covering the blister, but you need sufficient room in your boot to do that. Leave the skin in place if you must keep walking, until the skin underneath has a chance to harden.

Take your boots and socks off frequently when you are hiking, especially if the weather is warm and your load heavy, which puts a lot of pressure on your feet. Any break that is longer than 10 to 15 minutes is a good rule. It will help to not only discourage blisters from developing, but prevent your feet from aching as well.

When I was on the AT, I only took my heavy leather hiking boots off at the end of the day. I didn't want to bother and, at that point, I hadn't learned the wonderful benefits of releasing my feet from their prison. By the time I got to Maine, the tops of my feet were numb. The doctor said I had damaged my nerves by not taking my boots off. It took months until all of the feeling came back.

Stress Fractures

Todd and I both fractured the same foot as the result of hiking injuries. Mine was caused by repeatedly tripping over rocks that were obscured by vegetation, and from hiking at too fast a pace over those rocks. My foot began to swell to the point that I began to sleep with my boot on, because I knew it wouldn't go back on come morning if I did take it off. On the trail, it's often difficult to tell on the trail if an ache or a pain is something minor, something temporary, or a discomfort you shouldn't even express because you would sound like you were just complaining. Nearly every day on a long hike, something will hurt. You must listen to your body and try to decide what it is telling you. Usually it says, "Ease off me," in the beginning of a hurt. Whatever you are doing, it's irritating. If you continue to ignore your body's signals, it could become an injury, and serious enough that you'll have to abandon your hike.

My hurt foot slowed me down to a 4-mile-per-*day* pace. I was literally dragging it along like the dead weight of a tree limb. My good leg and foot were beginning to hurt, too, because I was favoring it. I had to get to a hospital. The doctor gave me two choices—to cast it and send me home, or wrap it and send me back on the trail. I chose the trail until I rammed it very hard and had to finally go home.

Todd fractured his foot on a snowy traverse. He was wearing crampons but the soft, wet snow was balling up between the teeth, taking away all traction. He fell and slid about 10 yards into a tree. The snow had melted around its trunk, causing a deep well to form. His crampon bit into the tree's bark and remained rigid, while his body fell into the hole, twisting and turning. He cracked his arch. He had to walk out 14 miles to a road where he and his buddies hitchhiked into town. They got to a motel and Todd soaked his injured foot in a trash can of ice. He, too, chose to try to continue his hike but had to abandon it, like I had.

Getting home with an injured foot was probably worse than getting out of the backcountry. Todd had to stand on the highway with crutches and a cast and a sixty-pound pack for hours. He couldn't take his pack off because he couldn't get it back on without help. Some people drove by pointing and laughing and making fun of him. It was very disheartening.

I, too, had to hitch and I extended my foot out in front of me so people who weren't normally inclined to pick up hitchhikers might feel compassion toward me. One motorhome that I flagged down for directions to the hospital wouldn't even roll down the window so we could talk. Instead, we spoke through the cracked open visor, they were so afraid of an injured young woman backpacker.

Stress fractures from hiking occur quite frequently. I read in a Maine register that a woman had to abandon her 2,100-mile hike at the 2,050-mile point because of a stress fracture. There is nothing you can do about a bum foot. I've seen folks continue backpacking with a broken arm in a cast after they fell, but not a foot. You must either get out of the backcountry by your own steam or get air-lifted out. Staying off your foot is the only way to heal it. My injury healed in two weeks. Because of the location of Todd's fracture, on his arch, it took months.

Snakes

The number-one most asked question when hiking the Appalachian Trail is, "See any snakes?" Some people are obsessed with snakes, so terrified of them that they refuse to even go into the woods. This is foolish, but not being educated about them is equally foolish. Whenever I see a snake, *any* snake, my adrenalin immediately surges through my body and I hop madly away. Then, from a safe distance of about three big steps, I look the situation over. I look at the snake's head. Except for the coral snake, all poisonous snakes in the United States have flat, arrow-shaped heads. If it has a rounded head, I relax and watch and study the snake. If it is poisonous, I respectfully let it go on its way.

When you are in the woods, look carefully before you place your hands and feet. If a log is in your path, place your hiking stick there first instead of your foot. I've sat down on rocks a half dozen times, leaned back on my hands, and heard a rattle. Rattlesnakes can be coiled up underneath the rock you rest on. When climbing over rocks, always be careful where you place your hands.

Think about the weather and the temperature of the day. Where would you want to be if you were a snake? I've seen them stretched out on a dirt road or the trail at the end of the day, trying to soak up the heat. But,when it's warm out, a snake is trying to get

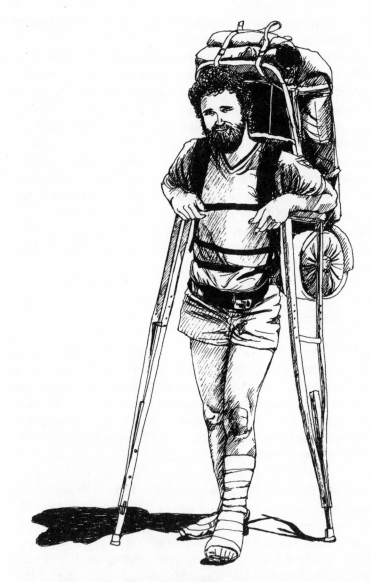

cool. Look out for them in shady spots under rocks, et cetera. Evening is when they are most active in the summer months. Not only is it cooler then, but they also hunt at night. Avoid walking barefoot to the spring or around camp if you are in snake country. Remember that the woods are their home. Respect their right to be there. Do not kill any snake unnecessarily. They have an important job of killing rodents and rats and preventing the spread of disease. If you give them the chance, they will more than likely move out of your way.

Most snake bites are caused by stepping on the snake or from getting too close to it. Only 60 percent of poisonous snake bites have venom injected in them. The snake may just have eaten.

If you are unfortunate enough to be bitten, there is some new research and advice on the treatment of it. Never use a snakebite kit to cut and suck the venom, says Maynard Cox, founder and director of the North Florida Snakebite Treatment Center, and the World Wide Poison Bite Information Center, and author of *Protocol for Emergency Room Procedures and Hospital Management of Snakebite*. He contends that snakebite kits are dangerous. He says, "The poison is walled in by itself in the capillary beds at the bite site for 12 hours." A tourniquet isn't necessary, because the poison isn't going anywhere.

Cutting through the fang marks can cause infection and damage to the muscles, veins, tissues, and nerves. Sucking only gets out 2 to 10 percent of the venom and only if it is done immediately. Treat for shock instead. When death occurs within the first 30 minutes after snakebite, it is from shock. If a victim survives the first 30 minutes, he or she will have 12 hours to get help. Victims go into shock because of the terror and the pain. A burning, fiery pain accompanies a bite and when it is located on a main artery or nerve trunk, the pain is greatly intensified. "If the face is pale, raise the tail. If the face is red, raise the head," Cox says. Do not allow the victim to get hot or cold. Get him or her to a hospital to get antivenin.

One more thing—don't be fooled into thinking that just because it is cold out, snakes will not be out. The weather has to get below freezing and not above 40 degrees Fahrenheit for several weeks for snakes to hibernate.

Insects

How "bad" bugs are really depends on your tolerance level. When we took our 4-H twelve-year-olds out onto the trail, they lathered on bug dope at the first *sighting*. They had so much on, they reeked when you got anywhere near them. Todd and I failed to even see an insect.

We judge the degree of insect severity by our experience out in the Sky Lakes area in Oregon. The mosquitoes were so thick we could not relieve ourselves without our partner waving a piece of clothing furiously in front of the exposed area. They bit us through our pile clothing and through our tent wall if you leaned your head against the nylon. When you dove into the tent at night, while the other flapped violently, no less than 100 got in with you by the time you quickly zipped up. Those were "bad" bugs. No insect experience has ever come close to that. We always think back to that time and say to one another, "These bugs aren't anything."

We go to every effort not to put on bug dope. We often carry a pair of very thin cotton long pants and a thin long-sleeved shirt if we expect the bugs to be bad in the evening. I cannot bring myself to wear long clothes while I hike unless it is cool or the insects are intolerable, like they were in the Sky Lakes. Hiking and sweating in warm clothes in warm weather seems to me like just so much torture.

We stay away from bug dope containing DEET (diethyl toluamide), again, unless they're horrendous. DEET is readily absorbed through the skin into the bloodstream and can be potentially harmful, especially to young children. We've seen it melt ballpoint pens in the hands of Maine trail surveyors. Our friend, Redman Breadman, took his plastic bag of bread and pressed it to his dope-covered forehead. The writing and design on the bag were transposed to his forehead. That's scary. What does it really do to your skin? What does it do to the food that you handle? Or, what does it do to a man's genitals when he relieves himself, because on the trail hardly anyone washes their hands before they eat or urinate. Rubbing poison on your skin sounds scary. If you do choose to apply it, keep it away from your face, because chemicals have a way of creeping. Your mouth, nose, and eyes are *no place* to have chemicals.

When we began having babies and taking them into the woods, we looked for an alternative. In the last few years, there are a few natural insect repellents that have entered the market. They often use natural citronella oils as their active ingredient to repel the pests. They seem to work quite well, but, like I said, we've not been in bugs as bad as those in Oregon, so we haven't really put the new repellents to the test. Head nets work fine and can be purchased at an army-navy store at a low price.

The big scare is Lyme disease. We probably know as many people who've had this as have had giardiasis. We read somewhere that certain New Jersey backyards were tested for the presence of Lyme disease and 45 percent of them, in this particular area, were infested. You don't need to go to the backcountry or deep woods to become infected. You needn't stay indoors either, for fear. The best thing to do is to educate yourself.

Deer ticks can be as small as the dot at the end of this sentence—unnoticeable. They are much smaller than the common wood tick, which does not transmit Lyme disease. You can take precautions like wearing light-colored clothing to make them easier to spot, and you can tuck your long-sleeved shirt into your pants, and your long pants into your socks or boots. You can search for them at your hairline, armpits, groin, and behind your knees, but all of this searching can make you nuts. My friend was bitten under his backpack shoulder strap and he had taken all of the above precautions.

Know the disease's symptoms: a bull's-eye-shaped circular rash with a clear center around the bite can occur from three to thirty days or not at all. What victims commonly complain of sound like flu symptoms: fatigue, headache, muscle and joint pain, and swollen glands. Since the peak tick season is May through July, which is *not* the flu season, if you have these symptoms and have been in an area where you could have been infected—wooded, grassy, or marshy areas—consider that you could have Lyme disease. If you can't find the bite and the symptoms continue longer than the flu would, get checked out by your physician for Lyme disease.

A friend of mine had headaches for a year and also felt stiff and achy all that time, too. She thought she was getting arthritic and was aging overnight, but instead, she had Lyme disease. Be aware of the symptoms. If any present themselves, consider that you may be infected.

PART IV

EXTRAS

▲ ▲ ▲ ▲ ▲ ▲ ▲ ▲ ▲

Taking the Kids Along

▲ ▲ ▲ ▲ ▲ ▲ ▲ ▲ ▲

I was once on a panel discussion at a long-distance hikers' gath ering, talking about why we love to hike and how it affects our lives. I remember getting choked up with tears and I found myself unable to speak. Todd and I had recently made a decision to drastically change our lives and begin a family. Nearly all of our friends who were serious hikers—and there were hundreds of them— were either single, married and childless, or older with grown children. No one was there to tell us how to continue being active in backpacking and bring our children along. No one was there to tell us that it could be done, or to encourage us. We were going into uncharted territory. I wish there had been someone there. We wouldn't have felt so frightened and unsure.

Since we have successfully toted our babes into the wilds, and enjoyed it, we are here to encourage you. Some of our serious hiking friends have since had children, but to our surprise, they have not ventured out with them. On one hand, we can understand. It is one of the most frustrating, trying, and exhausting things we've ever done. To me, the more adventurous of the couple, it is always worth it. To Todd, the homebody and packhorse of the team, he sometimes questions the value ... until it's over. Then even he talks about the difficult times with humor.

Take your children along into the wilds with you. It can be hard work, but think of what you will be doing for them. Think of how it will color who and what they become. Loving nature and the outdoors is one of the finest gifts you can give your child.

Backpacking with a Baby

When my daughter Sierra was born, I expected her to change my life. I was told I would be unable to do many of the things that I had done when I was childless. Every mother I knew had shared this piece of advice with me. But there were some things, my strongest needs and loves, that I was not planning on parting with. Yes, I would adapt and conform, but I would not abandon them.

Backpacking was one. With 12,000 collective miles of long-distance hiking between Todd and me, we weren't "casual week-enders" before parenthood; we were long-distance fanatics. And, as contributing editor of *Backpacker* magazine, I had begun to make a living from doing what I love most. Giving it up was out of the question.

But, I must admit, backpacking with a baby—taking a helpless, dependent infant on the trail—was enough to make even two seasoned hikers uncomfortable. The books on taking your children into the wilds that were in our library dedicated about one paragraph to infants—simply advising you to wait and not take them. Nor did we know anyone personally who could give us advice. We were on our own.

First, we needed to get a three-person tent. Then, find a good baby backpack. There are many on the market, but we needed the biggest, most rugged pack we could find. We narrowed it down to a carrier from a major manufacturer that could tote up to sixty pounds. We carried Sierra around the house and homestead anytime she felt the need to be right with us and we needed to get something done: when we canned fruit, cut up apples for sauce, mowed the lawn, trimmed the fruit trees, or ran the sweeper. She came to love being in it.

Our first try was the 60-mile Loyalsock Trail in north-central Pennsylvania. There are road crossings every 5 to 10 miles, in case we needed to bail out. Inclement weather or Sierra coming down with a fever were two reasons we would have abandoned our trip. And we knew she could also make us miserable by being grossly unhappy for whatever reason. If that were the case, we wouldn't want to continue, either.

We waited for a stretch of really good weather before departing, days of fair and sunny skies after a front passed through. If there is much rain in the forecast, more than a chance of showers, it is not worth going. We've learned that it is just too much to deal with and is too little fun. But to play it safe, carry extra food, clothing, first aid, et cetera. Imagine the worst scenario and plan on it. You must be ultra-responsible when you are taking a baby backpacking. You are not just dealing with your own well-being but that of your precious, dependent child. You must know your stuff and be a competent, experienced backpacker who has already been placed in a lot of situations.

The first thing we discovered once on the trail was that our pace and the amount of miles we could cover in a day would go down radically compared to what we were used to. Sierra was happy in the pack for about 60 to 90 minutes at a time—long enough for us to hike about 2 to 3 miles. After that, she needed to get out, but it was also time to change her, feed her, give her a drink, or merely let her stretch her little body. Half the time she napped in the pack; the other half she looked around. We liked to get her out before her "desires" became "strong needs" and she had to cry to get her point across. We thought it was important for her to associate her pack with pleasure instead of discomfort and unhappiness or we'd draw a fast close to our beloved sport. Sometimes we needed to stop for a break 5 minutes after the last one, so we could change her soiled diaper. In many ways, your baby is in charge of the day's agenda.

Getting back into the pack and getting strapped down was often met with protest, so we sang, "Old MacDonald Had a Farm," her favorite song, and shook rattles in her face, which we had tied to her pack frame on cords, while we slid her in. The distraction worked.

We could only hike until about 4:00 or 5:00 in the afternoon. By 6:00, her mood was deteriorating rapidly. It was simply too long for her to be in the pack. We were tired by then too, especially Todd, whose pack weighed up to seventy pounds. He had to carry most of the gear for three people, since I had Sierra on my back and her pack did not have a huge capacity. Backpacking with a baby is not something you can do solo. There's just too much weight and gear involved for one person.

Once in camp, Sierra was a breeze at the young age of four months. She was too young to crawl or walk, so we simply plopped her down on our foam pads, braced her with our clothes sack, and both went about setting up camp while she watched and smiled.

Nighttime can be the most harrowing. Our daughter, by nature, does not sleep much during the day. However, the gentle rocking motion of the pack easily lulls her to sleep and she finds herself restless and unable to sleep deeply at night because of it. Plus, her teeth were starting to bother her. Since I was breastfeeding, I had to nurse her back to sleep four to eight times a night. This got very old. I easily became sleep-deprived. Sleeping on a self-inflated air mattress did make it easier for me to lie on my side and nurse for long periods of time.

One thing that is very different from your life back home is that there are no "helps" like high chairs for feeding and rocking chairs for consoling crying babies. A backpacking tent is a very enclosed place to be when your baby is screaming 12 inches from your ear. Putting on your warm clothes, getting out of the tent, and walking

your baby up and down the trail in the middle of the night is not an attractive alternative, either. Especially when you're in a public campground where you can't let your baby's crying go on or she'll wake everyone up. We found nighttime dealings to be the most difficult because of this too-much-daytime-sleep problem.

Diapering was one of our biggest concerns before we left on our first trip, but we soon worked out a simple system. We use cloth diapers at home for many reasons, ecological concerns being number one, but they also make the most sense on the trail. We always had a few urine-soaked diapers hanging on the back of our packs as we hiked. They were attached with alligator clips from the hardware store. What we couldn't dry during the day we hung on a line once in camp and usually by nightfall all the urine-soaked diapers were dry and light in weight. Old, thin diapers that you can totally open up, which we found at yard sales, worked best for this. To decide how many to take, just be aware of what your baby goes through at home in a day and take a few more. Diapers with bowel movements in them were simply folded up and stashed in a plastic bag to be dealt with when we returned home. Washing diapers out in a stream is unthinkable. It would pollute the water. And to carry a large enough bucket to rinse them in away from the stream is impractical. If disposable diapers are used, you must never bury them but must carry all the weight until you reach a trash can, and they're found infrequently in the backcountry. We used diaper covers with velcro closures instead of vinyl waterproof pants, but the latter should work, too.

To wipe her bottom clean, we used baby wash rags, pouring water from our water bottle to moisten them. One rag was for her bottom, another kept separate for her genitals, and another for her face, hands, and body. They all hung on clips on the outside of our packs as well. It was hard to keep her impeccably clean in the bush and we worried about rashes, but we washed her well with every change (albeit with cold water!), and never had a problem. Pack a generous tube of ointment along just in case. On all except the warm days of summer, it seems unwise to strip your baby naked to wash her. Rely on sponge baths instead.

What kind of clothing to bring for Sierra was another big question. Normally, I keep synthetics off her, but cotton, which provides no warmth or insulation when wet, is not a good choice—except for summer days when her drooling and water spilling can keep her chest cool. Polyester pajamas with attached feet work wonderfully. I put the thinner ones on as long underwear, and a thicker blanket sleeper on top. With these there is no "gappage" between pants legs and socks to get cold. Two pairs of socks go on her feet inside her sleeper when it's chilly. The polyester wicks the moisture outside the layers. Cotton turtlenecks keep her neck warm and trap her heat inside. Much of your body heat is lost through your head, so a hat on the trail is very important for your baby. Remember, babies have very little thick hair to keep them warm and are exerting very little energy by merely riding. When it's cool, Sierra wears a hat all the time, day and night—a pullover with an enclosed neck and cut-out hole for her face. Short-sleeved cotton T-shirts are all that she needs when the weather is very hot.

It's sometimes difficult to determine how many layers of clothing your baby should be wearing. There is such a vast difference between your level of comfort when you are exercising and your baby's as she sits. I check her skin temperature often with the touch of my fingers: her nose and hands, the back of her neck, and her chest. If her limbs are cold under her clothing, that is a sure sign that she is quite cold and needs more clothing on.

Keeping her warm while she sleeps can sometimes be a challenge. We brought along some polyester baby sacks with legs in them that zip up the front and drawstring close around the head. She stayed in these fine when she was asleep but often got frustrated when she woke in the middle of the night and could not move or kick her legs. As a result, she often wiggled up and got her upper body out of the sack. We put an extra layer or two on her upper body to compensate. In the summer, we brought along synthetic blankets and merely covered her with them. One problem when she woke up crying was that her body temperature would rise the more upset she got, making her sweat more, be more uncomfortable, and give her more reason to cry. Taking off her hat and clothes to cool her left her perspiring head vulnerable to the cold and it was difficult to put it back on once she fell asleep. We tried not to let her cry too hard. If we did take her clothes off, we put them right back on once she calmed down but before she drifted off to sleep.

It's pretty uncomfortable to try to sleep with your baby inside your sleeping bag. To be warm yourself, you often need your bag zippered and closed to your neck. If you nurse, the baby's head is much lower and your bag would cut off her air. Plus, there isn't really enough room for the baby and you cannot move in your sleep like you need to. Her own sleeping space (three-person tent), with her own pad and sleeping gear, is essential for a good night's sleep for all.

As a backpacking parent, there are a few major things you must concern yourself with to insure your child's well-being. We know what to do for cold; what about heat? You must make sure your baby is getting enough fluids so she doesn't become dehydrated. When Sierra was young and nursing often, I offered my breast every time we took a break. Then, all her needs for nourishment would be met. If that is your situation, the mother must keep her body well hydrated or her baby's nursing will dehydrate her. Once Sierra got older, I offered her my cup of water every time we took a break. Sometimes she only needed a sip, but that may be all we adults need to quench our thirst.

For protection from the sun, she wore a sunbonnet whenever

the sun was out and warm. Her pack had an awning but the sun still poked in. We put thin, light-colored sleepers on her when hiking in the open sun out west when the air temperature was not very high. When her legs were exposed, we put herbal baby suntan lotion, bought at a health food store, on that part of her body.

Major protection from the rain is obtained from her pack awning, but we also use an umbrella and a pack cover; the kind of cover designed for an adult internal frame backpack works best. When hiking in forested areas, we use a fold-up umbrella. Tree limbs hang lower when their leaves are wet and the branches can hook under a full-sized umbrella and flip it back. You must lean into these lowered branches to prevent this from occurring. In the west, in the open, we use a large umbrella for greater protection. Umbrellas work well as a sun shield, too, but do not hold up well in the wind. We strap it to the side of our pack and carry it on the outside. On the trail, nursing in the rain can be a real challenge. Find a comfortable piece of ground, put your foam pad down, lean against the trunk of a tree, and prop your umbrella up over both of you.

Always carry some sort of fever reducer such as an aspirin-free pain reliever for children; I carry a tincture of the herb echinacea, which is a natural immunity booster, stimulant, and fever reducer. I put a few drops in her juice regardless as preventive medicine. I also bring along homeopathic vitamin C tablets for children if it's cold out. Babies stay amazingly healthy on the trail, as adults do. As long as you are getting enough rest, food, and drink, and are warm enough, the exercise, clean air, and lack of germs keeps you healthy.

After 300 backpacking miles of carrying Sierra, we feel pretty confident and comfortable with her on the trail. We've had her out in the cool spring, in pouring, nonstop rain, in bugs in the heat of the summer, in the desert sun, and in the chilly autumn. We found we could cope with nearly everything but days of steady rain.

As she went from four to ten months old, things changed. For one thing, she began to eat solid food. Fortunately, you can buy freeze-dried food crystals for babies in large supermarkets, including cereal, fruits, vegetables, and dinners. All you do is add water, stir, and serve immediately. But because she was eating solid food, she began to have bowel movements—up to four or five a day—and she often soiled her diaper cover and clothing besides. The amount of wash that she went through was amazing! That is one thing to be prepared for—lots of dirt. Babies make more of a mess, too, by rolling in it, rubbing their feet back and forth in it, et cetera. As she got older, Sierra was content for longer periods of time in her pack. She could see more and entertain herself more easily. She also fell asleep more quickly and with less coaxing, making our sleep at night, however, more and more frequently disturbed ... again, too much daytime sleep.

As she learned to crawl, we could not put her down just anywhere. It had to be dry and safe. The forests of the eastern United States were fine, but the desert canyons of the Southwest, containing rocks, cacti, and cliffs, were not. We had to take turns holding her. This was very difficult, for she now weighed twenty pounds, and it was very frustrating, for only one of us could do things in camp while the other idly stood holding Sierra.

By this time, you may be wondering if it is, indeed, worth it. It probably sounds like it is a tremendous amount of work and very inconvenient. But I have not told you the real reason why we go to all that work and tolerate the pain of carrying heavy loads (especially Todd)!

We have watched our baby's senses open wide to all the beauty nature has to offer. We have seen her stare, mesmerized, by sparkling sunlight on a lake. We have watched her listen to a singing brook and follow wind as it raked through the trees and fluttered the leaves. We have listened to her caw at ravens and be so delighted when they answered her back. We have enjoyed watching her discover textures like pine cones and big oak leaves and sand in her toes. When she wakes up in our tent, she immediately rolls over and smiles before her eyes even open. We know she is happy out there.

Coming back to our home convinces us, if we weren't already sure, because every time we return from a trip, she seems to suffer withdrawal and looks disoriented. She then has a carpet to sit on, instead of pine needles and dry oak leaves, and her mobile to watch, instead of the wind and the dancing sunlight. At home, she is separated from her beloved mother and father to a much greater degree. We naturally set her down to do our chores. This is a huge difference from the trail, where *both* of her parents are with her 24 hours a day and she is close to the rhythm, smell, and feel of our bodies. We can't be on the trail all the time, but we do take her out-

doors every chance we get and for extended periods of time. We're hoping that if she gets anything from these experiences, it's a deep love and respect for the earth and all wild things. Then, all the work will be worth it.

Backpacking with Children

When planning mileage for a trip with a toddler, a half mile per hour is usually a reasonable pace. Hike a short distance so that your child can walk alone. Always wear a child carrier for that last, crucial, tired mile back to the car.

Like adults, children get a boost from eating snacks throughout the day. Slices of oranges or a handful of raisins and peanuts will do much for their morale and keep them moving. Children cover a lot more ground than adults do, with their running back and forth, so be sure to pump plenty of water and juice into them to prevent dehydration.

In the summer, dress your children in 100 percent cotton, not polyester or cotton blends, which are hotter, less absorbant, and less comfortable. Dress them in bright colors, too, instead of greens and browns, so they will be easy to spot should they wander off.

Consider bringing along a friend for your child. The children will entertain each other, resulting in a better time for the adults, too.

Start out by day hiking before tackling an overnighter. You'll learn what type of terrain your children can handle, whether everyone is prepared for changes in weather, what you are carrying that you don't need, and what you have neglected to bring.

To provide extra warmth for a baby's or toddler's legs when he or she is being carried, slip adult-size wool socks over the shoes and up the legs. Pin them to prevent slippage and from getting lost.

It's a good idea to set up your tent in the yard before your first trip. Spend the night in it and even have your children take their naps in it so they aren't afraid in the strange, new place they are required to sleep.

A walking child may need a little help to step over rocks or maintain his or her balance on uneven surfaces. The parents can take a walking stick and each hold an end so it is parallel to the ground. The child can walk between them, using the stick as a handrail.

An adult's sleeping bag can be used for a child by simply folding the foot underneath for extra padding.

Young children should hike within sight of their parents, and older children within earshot, calling out often to report in. Plan to regroup with older children at any fork, turn, or major point on the trail, so no one gets too far ahead or behind. Your child should always carry a whistle and know the right occasions to use it.

Biking with a Baby

When Todd carried his ninety-pound pack up the desert canyon in Capitol Reef National Park in Utah for an *overnighter*—complete with diapers, two and a half gallons of water, and most of the gear for *three*—we knew it was time to shift to a new sport for a while. On that climb, he looked at me and said, "This has ceased to be fun." He looked so pathetic and I felt so badly for him. My own pack weighed about forty-five pounds but I could not fit any more into my child carrier.

"We'll get mountain bikes and a bike trailer and ride converted rail trails," we decided as we climbed. "We'll still day hike and camp, but we'll put the longer trips on hold until the children can walk." We liked the new plan, especially once I got pregnant and increased our family to four with the birth of Bryce. With two in diapers, backpacking was out of the question.

What further convinced us was the wonderful new tent we were now sleeping in: a five- to six-person tent, weighing fourteen pounds. Todd was depressed when he heard the weight, but I assured him he'd only be pedaling it on a bike or rowing it in a canoe. I proved to be a liar four short months after Bryce was born and we went out for an overnighter. Once again, his pack was soaring around eighty pounds and we could only hike a mile or two with Sierra walking.

We learned with Sierra that a three-person tent for three people, even if that third person is a baby or a young child, is tight. Todd originally thought we should take two two-person tents when our family increased to four, but I was not fond of that idea. I often have to comfort *both* children at the same time in the night, when one's crying wakes the other one up. They both want their mommy. It would be difficult to split myself in two. And what about the days of inclement weather when we must make camp at three in the afternoon because of rain? I'd much rather be with the whole family, playing and laughing and talking.

The fourteen-pound tent stayed and it proved to be invaluable on our first overnighter. Bryce awoke for the fourth time in the night and I had nursed to the point where I felt drained, physically and mentally, so I turned him over to his pop. Todd stood up easily, in the 6-foot-high tent, and gently bounced him to sleep. I saw him smiling in the shielded flashlight beam, happy for the space, because it was raining outside.

For our long bike trips, we use a bicycle trailer that was designed with handicapped children in mind, so their wheelchairs and themselves could be transported into the outdoor world via bicycle. It is much sturdier than most trailers and can take up to

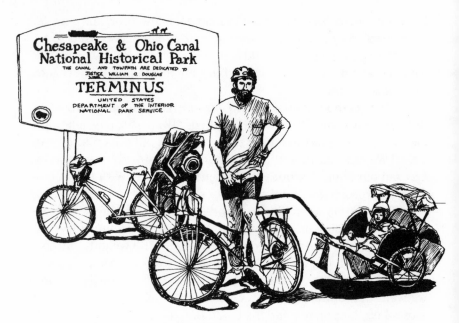

three children or just two with lots of gear. It has a tremendous load capacity, and can handle up to 150 pounds. For shorter trips we use a fold-up trailer; its light weight and portability make quick trips a cinch. While the children are young and infant Bryce needs to be in his car seat (because he can't sit up very well unaided), we bring both trailers.

Our first long bike trip was the 185-mile Chesapeake and Ohio Canal in Maryland. It's a flat towpath with many points of interest and it is off limits to cars. As backpackers, we were not used to dealing with automobiles on the trails and they made us feel uncomfortable, with our children behind us on the roads. Every 5 miles on the towpath, there is a camping spot with a picnic table, pumped water, and a latrine. Since the towpath paralleled the Potomac River, we swam about two to three times a day until we got closer to Washington, D.C., the southern terminus, and the waters became polluted.

Rain can be very difficult to deal with when you are biking with babies. Most trailers close up tightly to keep your child dry, but it may not keep him or her happy. If possible, schedule your trip after a cold front moves through and the forecast is a long stretch of fair weather. Once on the trip, it may be best to stay put until the weather clears, but your child may just surprise you and find the thunder and lightning and pouring rain on his or her vinyl windshield very fascinating.

Another thing that can be very difficult is dealing with hills. It is very strenuous to pull hills with a lot of weight (we had 100 pounds in the bicycle trailer), and riding downhill can be quite harrowing. There is a lot of weight pushing you along and you must really hang onto your brakes. Stick to easy, level terrain with only gently rolling hills. Pulling a trailer requires a different way of thinking and reading the road ahead and, hence, uses up more energy. You must be conscious of where the trailer's tires will run, aiming so rocks and roots are between them so the chance of it flipping is very low.

The most important thing to remember, for hiking and backpacking and all dealings with children, is to keep your sense of humor and to have fun. Your other alternative is to stay home and you and your child would be missing out on a wonderful and memorable experience.

For Todd and me, biking cannot come close to hiking and backpacking. But we have discovered some marvelous places to ride by joining the Rails to Trails Conservancy. The bike trails should hold us over until the kids can walk and we can get back into the wilderness and mountains, our true love. But there is nothing like seeing that contented happy smile on my husband's face as his bike and loaded trailer roll along almost effortlessly. We both know that would not be the case if it were all on our backs.

CHAPTER 10

Bringing Back More of the Outdoor Experience

▲ ▲ ▲ ▲ ▲ ▲ ▲ ▲ ▲

Journal Writing

If it weren't for our trips into the great outdoors, many of us would be seeking professional help. We look forward to our outings, our journeys, for months, years, and, sometimes, a big chunk of our lifetime. Dreaming and planning is often what keeps us plugging through the rest of our working days until we can once again make the great escape.

It's no wonder the camera is a standard piece of gear on even a day outing—an attempt to make the moment live long after it's over.

But what about the humble journal? Why do so few throw in a notebook when they're packing for a trip? It's lighter than a camera, especially with extra lenses, less bulky and fragile, and the price can't compare. Perhaps because, to many people, the thought of racking their brains after a physically fatiguing day to come up with something important to say, or anything at all to say, seems too much like work.

Why Bother?

Nothing can compare to that magnificent scene blown up on a projector screen. But you can't take pictures of smells, or sounds, or

182

tastes. Feelings and emotions are hard to capture on film. Conversations are, too. You can't trust your memory to keep these experiences alive.

You write so you don't forget things that moved you, lifted you, brought tears to your eyes, pain in your heart, intense beauty, severe hardship. These are the times of your life.

There are journals that tell only of how many miles the writer walked, where they camped, how many deer they saw. And there are journals full of sights and sounds and smells and feelings. Words that help you smell those fragrant azaleas, or feel the bite of that cold, driving rain, or hear the wind in that pine forest. A camera can only record on its emulsion what it sees through the lens. But every other sensory impression is recorded on the emulsion of your brain and is there to be written down and remembered.

Journal Writing Needn't Be Painful

Nor should it be something to dread. You don't need to take a course in creative writing. You needn't concern yourself with rules of grammar, punctuation, content, spelling, form, or anything else. Anyone who's fairly literate can keep a journal. A good way to loosen yourself and become free is to write or imagine you are writing to a good friend—someone who loves you and accepts you. On one trip I wrote to my mother, who knows very little about the outdoor world. I was careful to make it as descriptive as possible so she could feel as though she were walking there with me. When I returned home I took the loose sheets of paper, put them in a spiral binder, and had my completed journal.

The most common complaint is, "I can't think of anything to write." To solve this, you need to get in touch—become aware of what is happening around you. You begin by practicing being where you are. Tune into what is going on around you. It will teach you how to not live in a fog, prevent your life from passing by you in a blur, and to build these skills and sharpen your senses, so you can go back to your other life in society and get more out of that life, too.

See. Hear. Smell. Feel. *The moment itself* becomes more intense, more vivid, and more lasting as you pay closer attention. As you notice these things and write them down, they become part of your person. When you write about how the light looks on water, the laughter in the loon's call, the crispness of the air, you will come to possess these qualities in yourself for having noticed them.

Learning to See

Your first step is learning how to see. You can walk hundreds of miles, do a lot of looking, but actually see very little. You need to learn to see all over again. Notice details. Thoreau said:

> *We cannot see anything unless we are possessed with the idea of it. Many an object is not seen, though it falls within the range of our visual ray, because it does not come within the range of intellectual ray, i.e., we are not looking for it. The scarlet oak must, in a sense, be in your eye, before you go forth.*

Say you decide to look for birds today, or patches of color, or just things moving, and you spend your day looking for it. That's all you will see. Everywhere! You won't believe there were so many birds, or such a variety of color in a green woods, because you actually never looked for it. Describe what you see. Write it down in detail!

> *It is the most beautiful day of the year. At 4:00 the eastern sky is a dead stratus black flecked with low white clouds. The sun in the west illuminates the ground, the mountains, and especially the bare branches of the trees. So that everywhere silver trees cut into the black sky like a photographer's negative of a landscape.... The mountains are going on and off like neon lights. Clouds slide east as if pulled from the horizon, like a tablecloth whipped off of a table. The hemlocks by the barbed wire fence are flinging themselves east as though their backs would break.*
>
> —Annie Dillard, *Pilgrim at Tinker Creek*

What an image this creates in your mind! You weren't standing there with Annie Dillard but you certainly imagine you were. You can actually *see* the whole scene in your mind and it reminds you of days you yourself have experienced.

She is merely writing about the sun going in and out behind clouds and the wind hitting the trees. But look at how she describes the scene, look at her similes: photographer's negative, neon lights, a tablecloth. Draw from your own vast experiences to describe what something reminds you of. Paint pictures with words. When you record a day or a moment like this, and read it years later, you will be transported back and live it once again.

Learning to Hear

Listening is a lost art. Our lives are filled with static sounds. Radios in the background. Traffic in the streets. Phones ringing in the office, television in the next room. You learn to shut the sounds out, especially if you live in a city, or you wouldn't be able to sleep, or think, or have any peace at all. But tuning these sounds out also tunes out other sounds—good sounds, sounds that heal you, sounds that lift you. You even lose the ability to hear your comrades speaking and really know what they are saying. When you go into the woods, on your outdoor excursions, you need to pay special attention to this muffled sense.

> *Going up the hill through Stow's young oak woodland, I listen to the sharp, dry rustle of whithered oak leaves. This is the voice of the wood now. It sounds like the roar of the sea and is enlivening and inspirited like that, suggesting how all the land is sea-coast to the aerial ocean. It is the sound of the surf, the rut of an unseen ocean, billows of air breaking on the forest like water on itself or on sand or rocks. It rises and falls, wells and dies away, with agreeable alteration as the sea surf does. It is remarkable how universal these grand murmurs are, the backgrounds of sound, the surf, the wind in the forest, waterfalls, et cetera which … are essentially one voice, the earth voice, the breathing and snoring of the creature.*
>
> —Henry David Thoreau, *Journal*

Learning to Smell

Odors and fragrances are perhaps the most difficult sense to capture in words. There is the sweet smell of basal forests in the North woods, the smell of the river, fish. You ascend out of a damp, lush gorge with smells of musty rocks and moss hanging on your mind, to the open summit, where the sun bakes the exposed rock and the smell of heat predominates. Smells are most capable of bringing back floods of memories and all sorts of sensory impressions associated with that smell.

It was the smell of boiling potatoes that brought me back to the present. Now boiling potatoes cannot by any stretch of the imagination, be said to give off an ecstatically delightful aroma. But the moment I became conscious of the heavy odor wafting past on the clean desert air I experienced a sudden spasm of pleasure. ... All at once I was reliving a hundred dinners cooked in this same pot on this same stove while I leaned back, just as I was leaning now, against air mattress and pack. I found myself remembering warm desert valleys with the sun's afterglow still reddening distant hills, and damp, dark forests with the tree trunks flickering mysteriously into and out of an uncertain firelit existence, and cold, invigorating mountaintops on which I cooked and lived and slept and thought far above the petty world of men.

—Colin Fletcher, *The Complete Walker III*

Learning to Feel

All of the things that are happening in the natural world you are passing through affect how you feel, affect your body, your skin, how you feel inside—your heart and mind. As you travel through an environment and learn to notice all this external stimuli, think of how it affects you *personally,* internally, your mood, your thoughts and feelings it conjures up. The hot sun that cooks the earth is cooking your body, too. How does it make you feel? The rain that drenches the land falls on your stiff, cold body, too. How does that feel? What you are feeling is often in direct relationship to what is going on around you. Once you tune into the external happenings bombarding your senses, focus inside and discover what it is doing to you as a person.

He could feel the curve of his lips tightening in the dryness. He took off his clothes, all of them...

He removed his shoes. He lay on his back in the hot water, his toes grazing the shallow, sandy bottom of the pool. He could hear the water lapping at the entrance of his ears, the weight of water pulling on his flesh, settling on the bottom of the pool; he could feel the water prying at the layers of dried sweat. ... He climbed out of the pool and walked. ... The wind began to evaporate water and his pores closed like frightened mussels and trapped the warmth beneath the skin.

—Barry Lopez, *Desert Notes*

Using Analogies and Similes

We've all had experiences and associations in life. Draw on them to help you describe what you are writing about. Think of what it reminds you of. Compare it or contrast it to something else.

> *I have stood...listening to a queer vibration in the air and in the ground under my feet, like a freight train coming down the grade....*
> *A wall of water. A poor image. It looks rather like a loose pudding or a dense, thick soup, thick as gravy, dense with mud and sand, lathered with scuds of bloody froth, loaded on its crest with a tangle of roots.... It advances in crescent shape with a sort of forelip about a foot high streaming in front, making hissing, sucking noises like a giant amoeba, nosing to the right and nosing to the left as if on the spoor of something good to eat. Red as tomato soup or blood it came down on me about as fast as a man could run.*
>
> —Edward Abbey, *Desert Solitaire*

Look at the words he uses to describe water. Words you wouldn't normally associate with water, but that work wonderfully: freight train, loose pudding, gravy, blood, forelip, amoeba, tomato soup. Each analogy helps you to get the picture even clearer in your mind.

Describing People—Dialogue

The natural world you are traveling through isn't the only world you need to record. Your traveling companions make up a very important part of the whole experience. Recording the human element, what they looked like, acted like, dressed like, rounds out the whole experience.

> *We are both taking on the coloration of the river and canyon, our skin as mahogany as the water on the sandy side, our clothing coated with silt, our bare feet caked with mud and tough as lizard skin, our whiskers bleached as the sand—even our eyeballs, what little you can see of them between the lids, have taken on a coral-pink color of the dunes. And we smell, I suppose, like catfish.*
>
> —Edward Abbey, *Desert Solitaire*

Sometimes your excursions bring you into towns where you may meet people worth recording.

In a bar in Louisiana...

Next to me, a lady nearing her seventh decade kept
between us a white purse big enough for a mugger to hide
in. She wore a black wig. Her devil-may-care red lipstick
had come unhitched and slipped a notch; her layers of nail
polish were chipped like paint on an old dory; and her
hands lay in two piles on the bar, the slack skin taken up by
plumpness. As for the Jungle Gardenia perfume, it was only
a question of time before the tsetse flies hit.
... I heard the band through my elbows on the bar,
heard them against my forehead. The guitarist took off his
shirt and flaunted a curved chest white as the gut side of a
catfish. He was singing. I knew that because his mouth
opened and closed and he wasn't eating.
—William Least Heat Moon, *Blue Highways*

Try to capture pieces of dialogue. Dialogue that tells much
about the person just from the words they're saying.

In a parking lot six boys squatted about a Harley Davidson
and talked as they passed a can of beer. ... I asked one
wearing a BORN TO RAISE HELL *T-shirt what there was to do on*
a Friday night. "Here?" Everybody laughed. "You got your-
self a choice. You can watch the electric buglight at DQ.
That's one. Or you can hustle up a six-pack and cruise the
strip. That's two. And three is your left hand, a boy's best
friend."

"Maybe there's a tent revival or something like that."

"Heh! How do you revive the dead?"
—William Least Heat Moon, *Blue Highways*

Journal Hints and Tips

So you have learned how to use your senses. You have learned
how to listen to dialogue and notice people. Here are some parting
tips to get you started.

Ask yourself questions. Brainstorm. Notice everything. Feel
that cookkit jabbing you in the back through your internal frame
pack because of your haste to pack this morning. As you sit at a
view, be aware of the sun beating its heat on the nape of your neck,
the grit scraping your thighs on the rock you sit on, the cooling

sensation on your back as a breeze hits your cotton shirt, damp with perspiration.

When the woods are fogged in with rain and clouds, distances aren't clear, views are socked in, no grand, sweeping vistas encouraging broader thoughts, realize this closeness drives you into yourself. You think more, about soggy, coated nylon, stringy, wet hair, numb hands, home, loved ones, comfort, warmth. Realize that external conditions often dictate your internal thoughts. Then write them all down. Every little detail. Quickly! Just being aware of these things throughout the day will help you find more to write about at the end of the day. And it will actually be fun. Try to jot down some notes during the day, too, and when you take breaks.

You want to write down the pieces of your day. The moments. The patches. Details. Nothing is unimportant. All together they will capture the whole essence.

If you have trouble beginning, choose an extreme condition to write about—paddling up a river in a head wind, walking through a driving snowstorm. Choose conditions that are radical, extreme, so the obvious is very clear. After practice, you'll be able to write about subtleties.

Added Benefits of Journal Writing

Realize you are involving yourself in a creative act. Whenever your imagination, your feelings, and your intelligence work together, you are creating. And everyone's life, no matter what their occupation or state of being, can benefit from possessing more creativity.

Since you are getting in touch with your feelings and your world, you will know yourself better and this will help you communicate to others in your life.

Sometimes you wonder if you aren't standing still. You wonder if any personal growth is occurring, any evolution toward becoming the person you want to become. If you jot down your dreams in your journal and return years later, you'll find many of them manifested. This will give you courage and strength to continue striving because here in your journal is proof that you are indeed progressing.

And lastly, it teaches you to live in the present. Being aware of what is going on outside and inside creates a healthier attitude in which to conduct your life. How this present moment is the only moment you can affect, the only moment that matters.

"To affect the quality of the day," as Thoreau said, "which will in turn affect the quality of all our days to come." Isn't this, after all, what we go out there to do?

Photography

There are many good books available on the subject of outdoor photography, written by writers with much more knowledge than myself. But I will tell what I've learned, which are simple basics, in case you don't want to get bogged down with too much technical information.

Take pictures of people, not just scenery. Unless a scene is spectacular, shots of vistas and views can tend to look alike once you develop them. We experienced this on the Long Trail in Vermont. The summer days were either overcast or hazy and humid, the views were flat and colorless, never clear and crystal blue like a typical western sky. We soon grew bored with the slides ourselves.

Capture the life of the trail—stirring the supper pot, patching blistered heels. Move in close to your subject for portrait shots.

Don't neglect the emotions of the trail—a hiker's closed eyes and parted lips as he rests after a hard climb, sweat streaming down his temples; faces peeking out of rain jacket hoods; feet sloshing through mud and puddles.

Remember to turn your camera for vertical shots. If your subject is standing and fills the frame, it would make a much nicer vertical photograph than horizontal. It is difficult to take a really good picture at high noon when the bright direct sun is washing out the landscape. Morning and evening light is the most beautiful and makes the most successful shots. Overcast is the best condition for a portrait shot, where you don't have to deal with extreme light and dark shapes and angles. Avoid shooting a figure when the sun is behind him or her unless you are an experienced photographer and you can make your camera behave the way you want it to, to create a specific effect. Automatic cameras do not allow you to do this.

Remember that the slower the film speed (the lower the number of the speed—ASA 25 to 1600), the more light you will need. I found that anything lower than ASA 200 in the forest really limited what I could shoot without a tripod. So many of the deep woods shots had to be sadly bypassed when I had my favorite ASA 64 film in my camera. On our hike through the Cascades, I toted my collapsible tripod to capture all the mosses, mushrooms, and colorful lichens of the rain forest. Todd exhibited extreme patience, standing waiting in the rain, while I laid on the soggy earth to focus my camera in and wait for my lens, fogged from my breath, to clear. My camera had been broken before I left on that trip—the shutter was sticking and the repair shop never fixed it. Consequently, nearly all those belabored close-ups didn't come out but were washed out and overexposed. Todd was as upset as I was.

Anytime there is bountiful light—high, open country or desert—ASA 64 works beautifully. The color and clarity are remarkably different than, say, ASA 200 or faster. If you choose ASA 200 for your deep forest hikes and use Kodak film, go with Kodachrome instead of Ektachrome, which is a much "cooler" film. It accents the blues and greens and, God knows, the deep forest has plenty of blues and greens already, between the foliage, water, and sky. Warm Kodachrome will add much more warmth to your pictures— more reds, oranges, and yellow glows—a nice contrast to the already cool forest.

Use a polarizing filter for snow, water, open skies. It will protect your skies from looking washed out and water and snow from being too glaring.

When putting together slide shows of your trips, take some time to edit your slides. Weed out the mediocre ones, as painful as it may be. You want to spark your viewers' interest, not put them to sleep. Don't advance the frames so quickly that viewers can't grasp what you are trying to share in the slide. Aim for at least 4 to 5 seconds per slide, preferably more. Combine scenery with portraits and close-ups to add variety. Segment a few horizontals in a row and then a few verticals.

Carry more film than you think you'll need, and use it freely. Experiment with exposure and take photos of everything. Keep a record of what frames were exposed under what conditions so you can learn from your mistakes and triumphs. For its weight, bulk, and cost, film is a cheap accessory in helping you remember the magic of the trip.

On very hot days, put camera film inside your pack, away from the heat of the sun. Pack plenty of spare batteries and lens tissues. To be ready to take photos on short notice, wear your camera hanging from a thick strap against your chest, and cover it with a plastic bag in inclement weather, or carry it in your fanny pack, worn in the front, in a plastic bag.

Keep lens and filter clean so you can shoot into sunlight without a haze of dust ruining the shot. Remember that in rainy or dusty conditions you're going to need a lot of lens tissues. If you prefer to pack your camera, wrap it in a spare shirt or pair of pants, and stash it deep inside your pack where it won't get clunked. You will be less likely to go to all the effort to pull it out and you will miss an awful lot of good pictures.

11

Reentry: Coping with Coming Home

▲ ▲ ▲ ▲ ▲ ▲ ▲ ▲ ▲

*I never imagined how strongly the end would hit until it
happened. When I reached the summit of Mount Katahdin,
the northern terminus of the Appalachian Trail (AT), I
began to cry—tears of exhaustion, happiness, uncertainty of
the future. After two hours on the summit, I headed south,
down the roads that would take me out of the woods and
into the so-called real world. I did not want to go.*

—2,000-miler's journal, 1988

*R*eturning home is often the most difficult part of long-distance
hiking. You have grown outside the puzzle and your piece no
longer fits. The fast-paced, money-making society that makes our
country tick no longer feels natural. On the trail you come to discover that you don't need a lot to be happy. Not much money but
a whole lot of time. Your lifestyle was pared down to essentials
but was free. Now you have to adjust to other people's rules, the
absence of things you've grown to love, and the overabundance
of other things you would rather not be bothered with. There is a
definite feeling of loss, of displacement, of being out of your environment.

When I returned home from the Pacific Crest Trail in 1982, I
slept in the open air in the backyard, ignoring street lights. My parents murmured, "I don't understand it. She has a perfectly good
bed." I walked around sniffing a box of sage from my mother's herb

shelf because the fragrance reminded me of my days in the desert. I was haunted by memories, smells, scenes, feelings. I wore my tattered trail clothes, patched with whatever cloth I could find (usually worn-out rag socks), constantly. In them, I felt most comfortable. They reminded me a little longer of where I just was and reminded others that I was wanting to fit in, not yet, if ever. Because, if I took them off of my body, my mother would have quickly thrown them in the trash, for she threatened so.

Though books and classes on how to hike abound, there's nothing said on coping with the return, which can be as dramatic and emotional as the journey itself. All information is focused on getting you out there and moving you along the trail, but the move into concrete wilderness seems less welcoming and more hostile than the natural wilderness you just left. At the hostel I run for long-distance hikers on the Appalachian Trail, I left surveys for hiker's comments. As I was concerned about this problem of reentry, I wrote to some who had recently finished their long journey and returned home. I hoped to gain more insight into this difficult period and use it to help others who may find themselves in the same situation. One returning thru-hiker reports, "I was very tired and unenergetic for weeks and had a hard time controlling my eating. Driving a car was frightening—such rapid speeds and such mass confusion at rush hour."

Another said, "I'd forgotten how to dress. I used to be a bit of a clotheshorse, but they're no longer important to me. When I first got back I could not abide the noise of TV, or the radio, and even a lot of my family's voices. My tolerance for noise was almost nil."

One of my biggest problems was returning to my parents' home as an adult. It was wonderful to have a place to regroup in the interim period, but my father's and my priorities never seemed more distant. He became very annoyed when I left a kitchen cabinet door opened or stepped over lint in the carpet without picking it up. He could not believe I did not see it. My eyes were not accustomed to such details, if they ever were, and it didn't seem important enough to get upset over.

What makes the adjustment worse is that no one understands what you have just gone through. They don't see the changes that occurred inside you. They just see someone who wears their scummy, old trail clothes, still doesn't have a job, and has very strange behavior.

"The worst thing about going back for me was I had no one I could talk to about the trail. It was like a person inside of me wanting to get out. I think others care but I guess it's like a soldier returning from war; only he and his buddies know what it was like out there. It was and is our world."

One thru-hiker met with three kinds of reactions from people: "There were those who couldn't get beyond their awe, as if we performed a superhuman feat. There were the nuts-and-bolts people who peppered us with questions about equipment brands and logistics. There were few, very few people who seemed to be interested in what goes on in your heart and soul."

And another complained, "They all have such an elevated idea of what hiking for six months means. They don't want to hear about the hardships and how overcoming them was a very important part of the trip. And just how emphatically can you say, 'It was beautiful' so that they'll understand the other part? I preferred to keep my thoughts to myself."

Here lies much of the returning hiker's frustration: wanting to share what he or she has experienced so others can know and understand what took place on the trail and what is happening to him or her now that he or she has returned. There really is no cluing someone in unless he or she was there. The returning long-distance hiker is often in a lonely world all by him- or herself.

Some returning thru-hikers may prefer it this way, enjoying their uniqueness since most are introverted by nature. But no one enjoys feeling out of his or her environment, as if he or she doesn't belong. What makes this period so difficult is you usually have to return to someone else's home and participate in their lifestyle until you decide where to go and what to do next with your life.

So how can a returning hiker cope? Part of dealing with the culture shock of reentry is just by being aware that it is going to happen so you know what to expect and what not to expect. One thru-hiker writes in his journal in Maine, two weeks from the end:

Autumn melancholy grips me as I near the end of my trip.
The leaves are changing; have I? Where will I live? What will
I do now? Where will I go? Many thoughts, many questions.

This is good. Questions like these will help you enter the last stage of your journey, after you realize that your goal is finally and actually within reach. If you haven't done so before, it may be a good idea to think about what may come next. Perhaps this is the first goal of such magnitude you've set in your life. But as the end approaches, all realize that they indeed have the strength and perseverance to go after other goals. At one of my last town stops on the AT, I learned I had lost the full scholarship from my art school. I remember walking back from the post office teary-eyed, but shortly afterwards, as we climbed out of the gorge, my partner and I rationalized. "You could go to school to learn to paint your entire life. There comes a time when you must start doing what you love." I had my first solo art show when I returned, painting scenes along the trail, and it was a huge success. Like adjusting and adapting to new weather conditions and changes on the trail, I applied these lessons for living to my normal life and found they worked there, too.

Think about what makes you happy now, not before the hike, for there's a good chance you've changed. Try asking yourself questions like "What values are most important to me?" "What priorities are tops?" Your creativity may help you decide how you can take your talents, your interests, and your loves and find a way to support yourself. No matter who you are and what you return to, some money, sooner or later, will need to be made. In deciding how, realize your freedom and your free time will be of the utmost importance. Flexibility and independence will also be attractive and even necessary to your happiness.

Some of my survey hikers who planned on going back to their old jobs and did so were quite surprised to find that they were not as satisfied as they thought they'd be. One hiker who asked for a leave of absence instead of quitting outright said:

> *I took a management position which I absolutely did not want because my boss wanted me to and because I felt obligated. After four months being home, I've finally regained my senses and will return to school this fall as I had so carefully planned to do upon my return. I've kept asking myself, 'Didn't the trail teach you anything? How can you let all you've learned on the trail go to waste?' My answers to myself have helped me to decide to take the plunge and work toward a career I've wanted to study for six years. So maybe I did learn to 'go for it.' I'm just a slow learner.*

A thru-hiking anesthesiologist replies, "I find it more and more difficult to put up with the problems and egos of physicians that I deal with." An accountant is, likewise, very dissatisfied with the bureaucracy in his field. These professionals' values and priorities have changed while hiking and some sort of adjustment in their occupations is really necessary. If they adjust instead, they may be jeopardizing not only their happiness and peace of mind, but their integrity. Some acceptance of the ways of society is necessary for a returning hiker's survival, but it's a real sadness and a genuine loss to quiet your burning passion of wanting to change and make this world a better place to live. It's scary and perhaps even more courageous than it was to take that first step on the journey. The trail is over and society's demands for you to fit in are strong.

Besides your job, your lifestyle may also need to be altered. Perhaps it will need to be simplified, streamlined, to avoid things that devour your time and your life and keep you from being free and doing what you really want. You may find that you need to get rid of the TV so you go for more moonlit walks and read more books. Learning to say "no" and not joining the bowling league even if they need another member because you never liked to bowl may be good. Some folks in the outside world will call you selfish and not understand that you are taking care of your personal needs so you can be happy and peaceful inside. I've always believed, how could I be a good wife or mother or person if I am not happy and satisfied myself first?

You may feel a need to move to a more rural setting. Most folks cannot live in the woods for six months and not develop a need for wild, open spaces in their lives. Some stay away, claiming a weekend escape is only a tease. My one friend felt that, because of his new role as father and provider, he could not hike for any length of time again, so he burned all his trail guides and maps and gave away every piece of outdoor equipment. He pretends now that his wonderful hike never happened and is miserable for it. Don't deny yourself this life that has become a need. Go to the woods any chance you get. There is your home. If all you have is a few hours a week for a woodland ramble, you can make it enough.

After backpacking seven summers and reentering seven times, I like to think I have some solutions to the problem. Every time my husband and I return, we expect the coming home to get easier and usually it does. We get ourselves all fired up over our next goal, the next stage in our lives, while we're still on our journey.

Toward the end of our last trip, as we rested we drew floor plans in the dirt of the house we planned to build. We broke sticks into small pieces and designed our truss and roof system on lunch breaks. We were excited about being in the High Sierra but we were also excited to think of what we had planned next. Whether it's a move to a new area, starting a business, beginning a family, another trip, or building a home, we try to set ourselves up with a colossal goal to take the edge off returning. It usually works, although you will never glide so smoothly into the next stage of your life without some bittersweet feelings of melancholy and loss. Change is hard and something that you love is gone, over, so be easy on yourself.

Working with other people on maintaining or promoting the trail helps many post-thru-hikers. Others get together with hikers they've met on the trail or become involved with the Appalachian Long Distance Hikers Association and local clubs.

But perhaps your most valuable defense is to remember to keep dreaming. Keep reaching for higher goals. You must live your life for something that means the world to you. And realize that, like your journey, this displaced, confused state, too, will pass. Despite the difficult adjustments, I believe these long-distance hikers are much better, broader, beautiful people for the experience. It just takes some time to realize it.

One of the most profound illustrations of a change in me took place when I returned from the Pacific Crest Trail and learned that my father had cancer and only six months to live. He was young, and it shook our very close family. But I found myself becoming his nurse, his comedienne, his companion, since I hadn't yet entered the work world. When the cancer entered his brain, we'd chat about how much money I wanted to pay for the front lawn since he was dividing it all up before he died. My sister would enter the room and need to leave, our senseless discussion upset her so. As my grandmother wailed, "Why did it have to happen to him?" I instead asked, "Why should Daddy or anyone else be exempt?" Death is part of life, one flowing into the other. Where I had just come from, in the natural world, that was so blatantly obvious. My sister was ready to deliver a baby. It was clear to me that one life was making room for the next. I like to contribute my inner strength and understanding to the lessons I learned while on the trail. The strength I needed to work through the death of a parent came from the same source I tapped into to get through seven days of cold rain or a broken foot. From long-distance hiking, I knew what it meant to struggle, to have hard times, and knew even better that the storm would pass, the sun would come out, and I'd learn to smile again—believing in the continuity of life and living as though I believed it. If the trail gives us this, the adjustment period of reentry indeed seems minor.

Appendix

Freeze-Dried Foods in Bulk:

Stow-A-Way
P.O. Box 957
East Greenwich, RI 02818
(401) 885-6899

Wee-Pak
P.O. Box 562
Sun Valley, ID 83353-0562
(800) 722-2710

Mountain House
Oregon Freeze Dry, Inc.
P.O. Box 1048
Albany, OR 97321
(800) 547-4060

Alpine Aire
P.O. Box 1600
Nevada City, CA 95959
(800) 322-MEAL

Home Dehydrators:

Harvest Maid Dehydrator
Alternative Pioneering
    Systems, Inc.
4064 Peavey Rd.
Chaska, MN 55318
(800) 328-2853

Harvest Savor Dehydrator
Vita-Mix Corporation
8615 Usher Rd.
Cleveland, OH 44138
(216) 235-4840

BakePacker:

Strike 2 Industries, Inc.
E. 508 Augusta Ave.
Spokane, WA 99207
(509) 484-3701

Index

Other books you may enjoy from The Mountaineers:

Journey on the Crest: Walking 2,600 Miles from Mexico to Canada, Ross. A compelling narrative of a young woman's journey on the rugged Pacific Crest Trail. From the author of *A Hiker's Companion: 12,000 Miles of Trail Tested Wisdom.*

Wilderness Basics, 2nd Edition: The Complete Handbook for Hikers & Backpackers, by the San Diego Chapter of the Sierra Club, Schad & Moser, editors. Comprehensive resource covers all aspects of backcountry use: planning, equipment, navigation, weather; coastal, mountain, and desert travel; first aid, winter mountaineering, food, ethics, and more.

Gorp, Glop & Glue Stew: Favorite Foods from 165 Outdoor Experts, Prater & Mendenhall. Well-known outdoor folk share favorite trail recipes, humorous and practical. Highly recommended by *Backpacker.*

Mountaineering First Aid, 3rd Edition, Lentz, Carline & Macdonald. Fully updated; basic outdoor first aid. Conforms to latest mountaineering-oriented first aid classes.

Medicine for Mountaineering & Other Wilderness Activities, 4th Edition, Wilkerson, M.D., editor. Thoroughly updated and revised "bible," written by climber physicians for travelers more than 24 hours away from medical aid, and for climbing expeditions.

Hypothermia, Frostbite and Other Cold Injuries: Prevention, Recognition, Prehospital Treatment, Wilkerson, M.D., editor. Experts describe symptoms, solutions, and prevention. Includes frostbite and immersion.

Mountaineering: The Freedom of the Hills, 5th Edition, Graydon, editor. Over 225,000 copies sold! New edition of the classic text on climbing and mountaineering, from expeditions to ice climbing. Includes new material on winter and expedition climbing, and extensive updates to sections on equipment and belaying. Entire text has been re-vamped to include recent advances in technique and technology.

Available from your local bookstore or outdoor store, or from:

The Mountaineers Books
1011 SW Klickitat Way, Suite 107
Seattle, WA 98134

Or call for a catalog of over 200 outdoor books: 1-800-553-4453.

The MOUNTAINEERS, founded in 1906, is a nonprofit outdoor activity and conservation club, whose mission is "to explore, study, preserve, and enjoy the natural beauty of the outdoors ... ." Based in Seattle, Washington, the club is now the third-largest such organization in the United States, with 12,000 members and four branches throughout Washington State.

The Mountaineers sponsors both classes and year-round outdoor activities in the Pacific Northwest, which include hiking, mountain climbing, ski-touring, snowshoeing, bicycling, camping, kayaking and canoeing, nature study, sailing, and adventure travel. The club's conservation division supports environmental causes through educational activities, sponsoring legislation, and presenting informational programs. All club activities are led by skilled, experienced volunteers, who are dedicated to promoting safe and responsible enjoyment and preservation of the outdoors.

The Mountaineers Books, an active, nonprofit publishing program of the club, produces guidebooks, instructional texts, historical works, natural history guides, and works on environmental conservation. All books produced by The Mountaineers are aimed at fulfilling the club's mission.

If you would like to participate in these organized outdoor activities or the club's programs, consider a membership in The Mountaineers. For information and an application, write or call The Mountaineers, Club Headquarters, 300 Third Avenue West, Seattle, Washington 98119; (206) 284-6310.

About the authors:

Pennsylvania residents Cindy Ross and Todd Gladfelter are well-known hikers and the authors of many articles for outdoor publications. A contributing editor for *Backpacker* magazine, Cindy is the author of *Journey on the Crest* (The Mountaineers), as well as *Hiking: A Celebration of the Sport and the World's Best Places to Enjoy It*, and *A Woman's Journey on the Appalachian Trail*. Cindy and Todd also teach backpacking classes at a local college.